WATCHING WITH LINCOLN

And two other Plays

By

Michael J Shannon

Watching with Lincoln

By

Michael J. Shannon

Author's Note

By the time I came to write this play, I had some experience in this format, my JFK play, in particular, gave me the confidence to at least have a stab at it. What I needed was a context and that came to me during my research when I read about his second election; waiting for returns in the Telegraph Office of the War Department with a few friends and colleagues; reading from a satirical pamphlet, telling stories, and waiting to see if there would still be a Union when the night was over. It seemed made to order.

The only other thing I thought had to be in the play were excerpts from the debates with Douglas that touched on the slavery issue, the Gettysburg Address, and his final farewell to the crowd, which I expanded slightly to include a few famous lines from his Second Inaugural. I was helped with the structure simply because there was an historical record that included the timing of the returns, state by state, at first favorable and then not so much.

Of course, the occasion, Lincoln's impulse to talk, to entertain, covering his trepidation about the result of the election, offered an opportunity to reveal Lincoln more intimately. his innermost fears and hopes for the country.

"Watching with Lincoln" was first performed by Michael J Shannon at RADA Studios in London, in November, 2014. It was directed by Lora Davies and produced by Bolingbroke Productions.

Subsequently, a dress rehearsal of the play was filmed and can be viewed on Michael's website: micheaeljshannon.com.

WATCHING WITH LINCOLN

PART ONE

Setting: President's Room. Telegraph Office,
the War Department, Washington D.C.

Time: November 8, 1864. 7:00 p.m.

In the President's Room is a side table with writing
materials.. Next to it a WINGED BACK ARMCHAIR and
HASSOCK. Upstage right is a COAT TREE.

On the upstage wall hangs a LARGE FRAMED MAP of the
UNITED STATES, circa 1860.

The sound of RAIN LASHING and RATTLING windows,
together with intermittent TAPPING from the offstage
TELEGRAPH ROOM is heard.

THUNDER CRACKS as LINCOLN, wrapped in a cloak, wearing
a stove-pipe hat, and carrying a document case and a battered
umbrella, enters.

> LINCOLN
> Whoa! What a night! ,,, I thank you for coming.
> (dropping the case by the chair)
> They insist that I have someone with me when
> walking over here from the White House,
> though it's only minutes away.
> (crossing to coat tree)
> If I do come alone, which they hate, I am obliged
> to carry a cane or this tatty umbrella. Imagine
> anyone wanting to do me harm.

He hooks the umbrella on the coat tree and hangs up his cloak.

> LINCOLN
> It is a little singular that I, who am not a vindictive
> man, should have always been before the people in
> canvasses marked for their bitterness.

THUNDER CRACKS, LIGHTNING FLASHES.

> LINCOLN
> (shouting at the storm)
> "Blow winds and crack your cheeks! Rage, blow
> your cataracts and hurricanoes! Spout, till you
> have drenched our steeples, drowned the cocks!"
> … "King Lear". I take no credit.

He hangs up his hat and takes out a handkerchief.

LINCOLN

I learned that particular passage from Scott's,
"Lessons in Elocution", when I was a boy along
with a pile of others.
(dabbing his face)
But I'd never seen any of Shakespeare's plays
performed until I was president. Now I never
miss if I can help it.

He crosses to the side table.

LINCOLN
(picking up telegrams)
Let's see what Homer Bates has left me. Homer's
on duty tonight along with a couple of the other
boys. Doubt if there's much. Too early.
(glancing at a telegram)
Last spring I saw Edwin Booth in a trio of plays.
"Hamlet", "Julius Caesar" and "Richard the Third".
All very good. Though to me it matters not if
Shakespeare be well or ill acted. The thought
suffices.
(flipping through telegrams)
Four years ago I waited for returns with some of
you in the Springfield telegraph office, an
election that decided my presidential fate. Now
here we are again four years later in the telegraph
office of the War Department, waiting for returns
that will decide the fate of the nation. I make no
predictions.
(glancing at a telegram)
Indianapolis! 1500 in our column. Better than a
poke in the eye with a sharp stick. Let's hope
Indiana goes the same way.

He crosses upstage.

LINCOLN
We did well enough in last month's State elections,
took eight of eleven seats, twelve in Ohio.
(pointing to map)
But Pennsylvania was streaked with lean and that
state carries enormous weight...
(glancing at telegram))
This local feud between Governor Curtin and my
former Secretary of War hasn't helped. If you
remember, Congress was on his tail over some 'no
bid' defense contracts that may or may not have
benefited him. The Secretary may have been a loose
cannon, but certainly no thief. ... After he resigned,
I made him a Minister and sent him to Russia ... he
didn't stay long enough to unpack.

LINCOLN (cont'd)
(glancing at the map
A week later, or so it seemed, he was back in
Pennsylvania politics ruffling feathers…
(sifts telegrams)
Anyhow, this feud's hurt our ticket down there, so who
knows. Personally, I care nothing about re-election.
But if our divisions defeat us, I fear for the country.
(refers to map)
Two months ago I wouldn't have given a plug
nickel for my chances. Horrendous losses in the
Wilderness, Spotsylvania and Petersburg, left
me no choice but to draft a half a million men.
(sifting telegrams)
I was urged to postpone the call up until after the
election. Didn't do it. We must have the men.
(flipping another telegram)
Then it was suggested that the election itself be
postponed or cancelled. I never considered it. We
cannot have a free government without elections.
If the rebellion could force us to forego or postpone
a national election, it might fairly claim to have
already conquered and reversed us…. That position
scared the dickens out of some wealthy Party wags
who wanted me replaced on the ticket altogether.
Felt I was unelectable. Conjured up a 2nd Republican
Convention in Cincinnati with the idea of putting
General Fremont forward.
(pointing to map)
It came to nothing. Sherman took Atlanta and
Ferragut Mobile. So here I am, bent but not
broken. If I go down, I'll go down like the
'Cumberland', with colors flying.

He clicks his heels and salutes.

LINCOLN
I had hoped to get back to Springfield to vote,
but things being as they are I couldn't get away.
(glancing at map)
Not sure which way Illinois will go…. Four years ago I
was dubbed the "Rail Splitter Candidate". Now the
country is split and bleeding and many blame me….
I got that 'Rail Splitter' handle from my cousin, John
Hanks, who showed up at the State Convention with
two fence rails we were supposed to have split in the
Sangamon Bottom in 1830. I said I couldn't guarantee
those particular rails were mine, but I could guarantee
that I split rails around that time.

H crosses downstage.

LINCOLN

Even traded split rails for a new pair of trousers. I
believe the bargain was four hundred rails for every yard
of cloth. I must have split fourteen hundred and still
came up short. Those trousers barely reached my ankles.
(sitting in armchair)
The first thing Mary did after we were married was
to take me to a haberdasher to get me measured up
for a good suit…That set me back a hundred dollars.
And she's been spending ever since. But now she's
spending the government's money, redecorating the
White House. To be fair the place was looking a little
seedy after Buchanan left.
(slight pause)
Of course, that was in the early days before we lost
Willie to the fever. Twelve days after he was stricken –
he was gone…gone… It nearly broke me….

He tears up momentarily, then goes on.

LINCOLN

We have Tad, of course, who's eleven. And Robert
who I never see. Harvard. I did go there on one
occasion. Gave a speech. Think Robert was a little
embarrassed… proud too, I think … I hope…Trouble
was I was riding the circuit or at the courthouse with
various cases when he came to us. We saw little of each
other… so there's a distance, which I regret… After
Harvard, he wanted to enlist, was eager to join up, but
his mother wasn't keen… Finally, I asked General Grant
to find him a spot in the Army of the Potomac, which
he did.. Now Mary worries and blames me.
(laughing softly)
She'll – she'll - have to get in line.
(after a moment)
Still, the boy wants to serve and I don't blame him.

He rises and crosses to the map.

LINCOLN

When I was his age, in between careers, Black Hawk
crossed the Mississippi with 400 Sac warriors,,, wanted
to return to his tribal lands which had been bargained
away in what he then considered a bad bargain…. So I
volunteered for the 31st Illinois State Militia.
(moving down center)
The most pleasure and satisfaction of my life was being
elected Captain of that Sangamon Company of soldiers…
I guess you didn't know I was a military man. Yes, I
fought, bled and came away.

He chuckles.

LINCOLN

No, I was not at Stillman's defeat., but I was near the
place very soon afterwards. And it is quite certain I did
not break my sword, for I had none to break. But I bent a
musket pretty bad on one occasion. I had a good many
bloody struggles with the mosquitoes, and although I never
fainted from loss of blood, I can say I was often very hungry,
marching up and down both sides of the Rock River in
search of an illusive enemy.

TELEGRAPH CHATTER is heard offstage. Lincoln edges toward the chatter.

LINCOLN

I am just enough of a politician to know that there was
not much doubt about my nomination at the
Baltimore Convention. But about this thing I am far
from certain.
(listening)
I wish I were certain.

After a moment he turns to the "Watchers".

LINCOLN

I'll tell you who else was in that Black Hawk War, Jefferson
Davis and John Todd Stuart - Logan as well. Stuart was
the first to suggest that I take up the law. After I mustered
out, I got a copy of "Blackstone's Commentaries", had
jury duty on a few occasions, watched those lawyers, most
of whom were self educated like me, and I saw that it might
scour.
(glancing at map)
In time I walked or rode the sixteen miles over to Springfield
and plundered Stuart's law books... this was before he was
elected to Congress... I had given up the Black Smith idea
by then. Too much like hard work.

He chuckles and glances at the map.

LINCOLN

Of course, Lee and Grant both fought in our recent war
with Mexico. Now here they are in two different camps....
If I had any chance of being re-elected to Congress, my
opposition to that war cost me the opportunity. Judge
Douglas was still rubbing my nose in it years later during our
debates for the Senate. 'Spotty Lincoln' this and 'Spotty
Lincoln' that...reminding everyone, in case they had forgotten,
that I stood up in the House and challenged President Polk to
prove that we owned the spot on which the first blood of the
Mexican American war was shed...That put me in the soup
with the veterans and a string of others. Even my patriotism
was questioned.

He crosses down left.

LINCOLN

But when I made that challenge the war was nearly over.
Once we were in it I always voted to fund the troops. And
I stuck around Washington afterwards to help Zachary
Taylor, a hero of that war, be elected president.

He moves forward almost like an attorney in a courtroom.

LINCOLN

My point was a legal one. The Constitution gives war
making powers to Congress, not to the president. I
felt no one man should have the power to bring that
kind of oppression upon the country, especially over
disputed territory. General Taylor agreed with me.
    (moving stage right)
Yes, I know there are some who now accuse me of
executive tyranny because I instituted the draft and
suspended habeas corpus. But the situation is entirely
different. I am trying to save the country. President Polk,
a slave holder -
    (crossing upstage to map)
- wanted to extend slavery into new Federal
Territories gained from that war.... And now here we are,
years later, trying to pick up the pieces...It still pains me
to bring it up.

He moves right center.

LINCOLN

Mary's on edge... the election, Robert in the army, the
war, my safety, her safety.... She was returning to the
Soldiers' Home where we live in the summer months.
It's cooler than the city...
    (moving down stage right)
Well, the driver's seat came away, the horses bolted, and
Mary was thrown out of the carriage. She hit her head on a
rock and was poorly for a good three weeks.
    (sitting in armchair)
Her lengthy convalescence was partly fear I think.
She had convinced herself that the carriage had been
sabotaged. The bolts on the driver's seat were apparently
loose or had been loosened. But I find it does no good to
think on these things or we shall never go out.

He laughs painfully.

LINCOLN

She will just have to let Robert go, take his chances.... It's
Tad who could use the attention.

LINCOLN (cont'd)

Runs around the house pestering a Company of
Pennsylvania Bucktails quartered in the East Room...
along with his pet turkey who roams there on occasion.
Today he came rushing into my office. Wanted me to
watch the soldiers cast their absentee ballots before their
State Commissioner .We could see them from the window
all lined up. I asked him if his turkey intended to vote.
"No," he said. "He's not of age."
(tickled)
Not of age... eleven years old. He may not be
much with his books, but he's a quick witted lad.

Pause. Then, suddenly, he rises and strides toward the map.

LINCOLN

This whole thing may come down to the soldier's
vote. I did ask Sherman to furlough the Indiana boys
for last months state election, but didn't think it right
to extend their leave for this one.
(pointing at the map)
The general's marching through Georgia in a few days.
Can't hold him up just because it might cost me the
presidency... assuming the Indiana lads would have
voted my way.
(glancing at map)
We did furlough Federal employees here in the District,
freeing them to cast their ballots... Camps and hospitals
were emptied to do the same. And a government Steamer
was sent down the Mississippi to collect the sailor vote
from our gun boat crews. Someone said if there were no
other way, I would take a carpet bag and collect those
votes myself... Maybe not, but Mary might. She's that
anxious.

He momentarily studies the map.

LINCOLN

I am told the democrats expect McClellan to take two
thirds of the soldier vote in every State. Given the
choice between peace and war, they are betting the
soldiers will choose McClellan's peace platform.
(moving behind the armchair)
But I have been to City Point many times, talked to the
men in the camps and hospitals, and I feel they are
for their country, even if that means more war...
Frankly, I'd rather lose the election with the soldier
vote than be elected without it.

He crosses down left.

LINCOLN

Anyway, it is out of my hands. If the people support
the Union cause, they will act in the best interests
of the country and the world.
(sitting in armchair)
On the other hand, if they should resolve to have
immediate peace, even at the loss of their country and
their liberty, I know not the power of the right to resist
them.
(picking up document case)
It is their own business and they must do as they
please with their own.
(sifting through documents)
The decision they make will determine the weal and
woe of the nation.
(pulling out a document)
God knows I do not want the labor and responsibility of
the office for another four years, but I have the common
pride of humanity to wish my administration endorsed.
(taking glasses from his pocket)
And I want the opportunity to finish the job of putting
down the rebellion and restoring peace and prosperity
to the country.

He lays the glasses on the table and moves to the map.

LINCOLN

I think McClellan will probably carry New York,
Pennsylvania, New Jersey and Delaware, all the Border
States, and Illinois. That would give him a hundred
fourteen electoral votes.
(pointing to map)
I should get a hundred seventeen from all the rest,
possibly three more from the new State of Nevada.
If that proves to be the outcome, it will not scour.
The moral effect of such a close run thing would be
broken, and my power to prosecute the war and
make the peace would be greatly impaired. It would
be like having a gun to my head.

He steps forward with a wry smile.

LINCOLN

Reminds me of the occasion when I was accosted
by a man who actually did stick a gun to my head.
(raising his hands in mock fear)
"What's the matter?" I asked him. The man told me
that some years back he had sworn on oath that if he
ever came across an uglier man than himself, he'd
shoot him. "Well, shoot me," I said. "For if I am
an uglier man than you, I don't want to live."

He laughs at his own story and slowly ambles down left center.

> LINCOLN
> Even so, it was a close run thing. My improved
> countenance, such as it is, the jury is still out,..
>> (referring to his beard)
> I owe to an eleven year old girl from Chautauqua
> County, New York, Grace Bedell.
>> (sitting on the hassock)
> Grace wrote me a letter after I received my Party's
> nomination for president. In her letter she suggested
> that I might look better if I grew whiskers. I replied
> that having never worn whiskers some might think
> it a silly affectation. Still, I took her advice. And when
> my presidential train taking me from Springfield to
> the White House stopped near her village, I met Grace
> and told her my new whiskers were grown at her request.
> …I never asked if she thought it was an improvement.

He rises and straightens up.

> LINCOLN
> That was the high point of my thirteen-day train ride.
>> (moving upstage)
> The low point was sneaking into Washington after
> Pinkerton Detectives uncovered a plot to kill me.
>> (checking his pocket watch)
> The threat seemed genuine as it came from several
> sources. But I always regretted I let them talk me
> into it. It was a bad beginning, not at all presidential.
>> (referring to map)
> And it sent the wrong message to the Upper South and
> Border States that hadn't yet seceded from the Union.
> It made our resolve to resist the rebellion look shaky,
> and it made me look like a man more concerned with
> saving his own skin than saving his country, which
> was by then on the brink of war. If you recall, Federal
> forts, armories and other federal property had been seized
> by the Confederacy before I took office. Buchanan did
> nothing. That policy was untenable if the country were
> to survive.
>> (pausing slightly)
> The right of a state to secede is not open to debate.
> That question was settled in Andrew Jackson's time
> during the Nullification Crisis. No Sate can lawfully
> get out of the Union without the consent of the others.
> And no president can entertain a proposition for
> dissolution or dismemberment. "Disunion, by armed
> force," Jackson said, "is treason."

LINCOLN (cont'd)

The most important thing in my mind was not to start the
war, not fire the first shot, not shed fraternal blood. If we
had, I felt it would have led to the immediate dissolution
of the Union...We have not been enemies, but friends.
We must not be enemies...That the mystic chords of
memory, stretching from every battlefield and patriot
grave to every heart and hearthstone all over this broad
land, will yet swell the chorus of the Union was my
dearest hope.

He walks slowly down left.

LINCOLN

Now despite claims to the contrary we did not decide
to resupply Fort Sumter to provoke the Confederacy.
Nevertheless, our attempt to provision that Fort did
more service than it otherwise could have. Fort Sumter
was attacked and taken, leaving me no choice, but to call
out the war power of the government and so resist force,
employed for its destruction, by force for its preservation....
Loyal states were asked to provide 75,000 militiamen for
ninety days. I had no illusions the war would end by then.
But I never dreamt it would continue, as it has, for nearly
four years, with such a loss of life on both sides.
(smiling painfully)
Does it not strike you as more than strange that I have
been put in charge of prosecuting this war... when I
am a man who couldn't cut the head off of a chicken...I
did shoot a turkey when I was eight, but thereafter never
shot any larger game. For some reason I couldn't bear
cruelty to any animal. I remember giving the boys hell
for putting fire on the backs of turtles just to watch them
crawl from their shells.

He sits in the armchair and puts on his glasses.

LINCOLN

I sometimes feel like one of those turtles, catching fire
from all quarters. But I mostly manage to ignore the
threats, real or imagined, I leave it to others.
(picking up document)
I do have a pigeon hole in my roll top desk where I keep
all such trivia, read but not by me.
(reading document)
The country is not dependent on any one individual.

He quotes from, "Mortality", a poem by William Knox.

LINCOLN
"Oh why should the spirit of mortal be proud.
Like a swift fleeting meteor, a fast flying cloud
A flash of the lightning, a break of the wave,
Man passes from life to his rest in the grave."
(glancing up from document)
Now here's a boy due to be hung in the morning.

He continues reading for a moment.

LINCOLN
I think if a man had more than one life, a little
hanging might not hurt him. But after he is once dead
we cannot bring him back.
(looking up again)
It is not to be wondered that a boy, raised on a farm, in
the habit of going to bed of dark, when required to
watch, fell asleep?

He picks up a pen and dips it into the ink pot.

LINCOLN
My general's say I impair army discipline with my
pardons and respites. But it makes me rested when
I think how joyous the signing of my name will make
him and his family and his friends… So, the boy shall
be pardoned.

He signs the document, then blots it so the ink doesn't run.

LINCOLN
I don't always take the soldiers side. I recall a letter
from one who had been found guilty of stealing
forty dollars. He asked for leniency. Said he'd only
taken thirty.

He laughs and removes his glasses.

LINCOLN
Reminds me of the Indiana man who charged his
neighbor's daughter of unseemly behavior in having
three illegitimate children. "That's a lie," said the
neighbor. "And I can prove it. She only has two."

THUNDER CRACKS. The storm rages.

LINCOLN
A night like "Tam O'Shanter's Ride", the poem by
Robert Burns.

LINCOLN (cont'd)
(quoting Burns)
"The wind blew as twad blawn its last.
The rattling show'rs rose on the blast.
The speedy gleams the darkness swallow'd
Loud deep and long the thunder bellow'd.

He rises and comes forward.

LINCOLN
That night a child might understand
The Deil had business on his hand.
Weel mounted on his gray mare Meg
A better never lifted leg.
Tam skepit thro' dub and mire
Despising wind, rain and fire
Whilst holding fast his good blue bonnet
Whilst crooning o'er some auld Scotts sonnet."
And so it goes.
(pausing momentarily)
I had that dream again last night. I've had it before
Antietam, Gettysburg , Murfreesboro, and every
event of great national importance... I see a ship
sailing away, badly damaged. And our vessels in
close pursuit. I also see the end of the battle. The
enemy routed.... When I told Grant about my dream,
his only comment was, "Murfreesboro was no victory."

He smiles ruefully. Windows rattle.

LINCOLN
After Willie passed, Mary looked for comfort where
she could find it. One of the things she latched on
to was spiritualism. She even had séances in the White
House and persuaded me to come along on one occasion.
Said Willie spoke to her. I wasn't convinced... but could
see it relieved her mind.
(crossing upstage)
I do have one presentiment... that I shall not last the
rebellion. But that is another matter.

TELEGRAPH CHATTER and the TINKLING of a BELL is heard. Lincoln
turns to go, then quickly retrieves the 'Pardon" from the side table.

LINCOLN
Better have Homer wire this boy's Regiment or my
Pardon won't be worth much.

He goes quickly off. Lights dim momentarily. The sound of Telegraph
chatter and a CLOCK TICKING fill the air.

"Watching with Lincoln"

Part Two

Lincoln returns with a sheaf of TELEGRAMS.
Lights come up full.

LINCOLN
(crossing to map)
Indiana is ours without the soldier vote! That should
take some of the sting out of losing Kentucky, which
is dead certain, but not surprising. I was born in
Hardin County Kentucky, it's true. But my family
moved to Perry County Indiana when I was seven. So
I am not altogether a native son and cannot fault
Kentucky for deserting me.
(checking telegram)
My father left Kentucky because he couldn't get a
clear title to his land and couldn't afford the legal fight.
Then too, Kentucky being a slave state, it made it harder
for small farmers like my father to compete. So he
just packed up and moved across the Ohio to Indiana,
a Free State. Staked out a parcel of land near Pigeon
Creek.
(referring to map)
I like to think that Pigeon Creek and Perry County
remembered me today when they cast their ballots.
(sifting through telegrams)
That first year was especially bitter because our only
shelter was a half faced camp enclosed on three sides
with the fourth open to the elements and no floor.....
Gray's, "Elegy in a Country Church Yard", summed us up.

"Let not ambition mock their useful toil,
Their homely joys and destiny obscure;
Nor grandeur bear with a disdainful smile,
The short and simple annals of the poor."

Reminds me of a poem I wrote after a visit to the grave-
side of my mother and sister in Spencer County. It's fairly
brief and shouldn't try your patience. Here's a sample.

"My childhood home I see again,
And sadden with the view,
And still as mem'ries crowd my brain,
There's pleasure in it too.

I range the fields with pensive tread,
And pace the hollow rooms,
And feel companion of the dead,
I'm living in the tombs."

Slight pause. He ambles toward the armchair.

LINCOLN

I learned all of Gray's "Elegy" as well as long
stretches from the Bible, Shakespeare, Burns
and Bryon. Recitation was the primary mode of
teaching in those days. But later I did it for my
own pleasure and once I had it, it stuck.
    (sitting in chair)
My Father was illiterate, but determined that I get
a good education. In his mind that meant readin',
writin', and cipherin' to the rule of three... I was
schooled off and on until I was fifteen, but it didn't
amount to a year altogether.
    (glancing at a telegram)
My mother could read but not write. If she had
survived the milk sickness I imagine I would have
had her vote today. Sorrow comes to all and with
the young it comes with bitterest agony because
it takes them unawares.... I believe I was nine.
    (another telegram)
A year after she passed my Father went back to
Kentucky and married Sarah Bush Johnston. My new
step mother brought three children, a spinning wheel,
furniture and a pile of books into our lives. "Aesop's
Fables", "Robinson Crusoe", "Arabian Nights". I
wore the paper thin plundering those books and any
others I could lay my hands on.... We cleared eighty
acres that first year; Roughest work a young lad could
be made to do; plowing, fencing, killing hogs....I never
did like to work and I don't deny it. I'd rather read,
crack jokes, laugh, talk, tell stories, anything but work!
Here's one that comes to mind.

He places the telegrams on the side table and rises.

LINCOLN

A circuit preacher rose in the pulpit and
announced his text: "I am the Christ whom I shall
represent today." About this time a little blue lizard
ran up his roomy pantaloons.
    (desperately slapping his legs)
The old preacher, not wishing to interrupt the flow
of the sermon, slapped away on his legs, expecting to
arrest the intruder. But his efforts were unavailing....
Continuing the sermon he next loosened the waistband
of his pantaloons and with a KICK off came that easy
fitting garment.... Meanwhile, Mr. Lizard had past
the Equatorial line of the waistband and was calmly
exploring that part of the preacher's anatomy which
lay underneath the back of his shirt.

He squirms wildly.

LINCOLN

Desperate, the preacher reached for his collar button,
and with one sweep of his arm, off came that tow
linen shirt. The congregation sat as dazed.
(slight pause)
Finally, one old lady rose up and shouted at the top of
her voice, "If you represent Christ, then I'm done with
the Bible!"

Slightly embarrassed, he laughs at his own story.

LINCOLN

No offense, I hope. Certainly none intended.
Although I don't belong to a church, a condition I
had to answer when I ran for Congress in '46',
(sitting and picking up telegrams).
I can promise you that I will gladly join any church if
its sole qualification for membership is obedience to
the Bible's statement of law and gospel.
(referring to telegram)
From Secretary Fox, crowing over the defeat of a
couple of opponents. Well, he has more of the feeling of
personal resentment than I do. Perhaps I have too little
of it, but I never thought it paid. A man has not the time
to spend half his life in quarrels. If any man ceases
to attack me, I never remember the past against him.

Slight pause.

LINCOLN

A woman once told me that her idea of a true religious
experience was when one was really brought to feel
the need of divine help, and to seek his aid for
strength and guidance. I had lived until Willie died,
without fully realizing these things. That blow over -
whelmed me. It showed me my weakness as I had
never felt it before…. I can safely say that I now know
something of that change of which she spoke….
(sifting a telegram)
I have been accused of being both an atheist and a Deist.
Neither are true. Although Washington and Jefferson
were both Deist's. Believed in a divine intelligence
governing the universe… I myself believe that there is
a natural law of harmony, and that in that law are self
evident truths.
(laying aside the telegrams)
I recollect thinking even as a young boy, that there must
have been something more than common that those
men struggled for.

He rises and moves to the map, checking his watch as he goes.

LINCOLN

Years before I came to this office, I spoke of the danger
to American political institutions being greater now
than it had been for the last fifty years. In previous
generations, when the outcome of the American venture
in self government was still in doubt, all who sought
celebrity and fame and distinction expected to find it in
the success of that experiment.
(moving forward)
But now such is not enough for men of ambition and
talent. Towering genius disdains a beaten path. It
seeks regions unexplored. It thirsts and burns for
distinction. And if possible it will have it, whether at the
expense of emancipating slaves or enslaving free men.

He points toward the map.

LINCOLN

I first saw slavery in Kentucky. And then again in New
Orleans when I took a flat boat down there with Allen
Gentry, twenty four hundred miles round trip, to sell his
father's goods. There I saw the slave market. And again
in St. Louis two years later, my cousin, Dennis Hanks
and I, saw men chained, whipped, and scourged like cattle.
(referring to map)
When I came to Congress in '47' the slave trade was on
display, an offense and embarrassment to our nation's
Capital. I introduced a Bill that would have allowed the
people to restrict slavery in the District, but it got nowhere.
It wasn't enough of an issue at the time. The country,
North and South, expected slavery to peter out.
(moving slightly D.C.)
That assumption was questioned in '54' when Judge
Douglas introduced the "Nebraska Bill" in the Senate. A
Bill that would, if passed, extend slavery into new federal
territories west of the Mississippi.
(referring to the map)
As you know that Bill was passed and it changed everything. What began as a necessary evil was now being
promoted as a positive good. Although volume upon
volume is written that slavery is a very good thing, offering
the slave security and real freedom, we never hear of the man
who wishes to take the good of it by being a slave himself.
(moving slowly down stage left)
That Bill was conceived in violence, passed in violence, is
maintained in violence, and is being executed in violence.
And I said as much to Judge Douglas during our debates
for the Senate. Those debates went on for hours of course.
But the slavery question was the eye of the storm.

Lights dim around Lincoln as he steps on the hassock..

LINCOLN

A house divided against itself cannot stand. I believe
this government cannot endure permanently, half
slave and half free. I do not expect the Union to be
dissolved, I do not expect the House to fall, but I do
expect it will cease to be divided. It will become all
one thing or all the other.
(slipping hands behind his back)
Either the opponents of slavery will arrest the further
spread of it and place it where the public mind shall rest
in the belief that it is in the course of ultimate extinction,
or its advocates will push it forward until it shall become
alike lawful in all the States, old as well as new, North
as well as South.

He puts his left hand on the lapel of his coat and gestures with his right.

LINCOLN

I have always hated slavery I think as much as any
abolitionist....I have always hated it, but I have always
been quiet about it until this new era of the introduction
of the 'Nebraska Bill' began. I always believed that everybody was against it, and that it was in the course of ultimate
extinction. The adoption of the Constitution and its
attendant history led the people to believe so. And that
such was the belief of the framers of the Constitution itself.
(referring to Douglas)
Judge Douglas looks upon this matter of slavery as an
exceedingly little thing. This matter of keeping one fifth
of the population of the entire nation in a state of oppression
and tyranny unequalled in the world.... He looks upon it as
something having no moral question in it, as something on
a par with the question of whether a man shall pasture his
land with cattle or plant it with tobacco.... It so happens
that there is a vast portion of the American people that do
not look upon that matter as this very little thing. They look
upon it as a vast moral evil; they can prove it as such by the
writings of those who gave us the blessings of liberty.
(slight pause)
Now for the purpose of squaring things with the Judge's
argument of 'don't care whether slavery be voted up or
voted down', for holding that the Declaration of Independence
didn't mean anything at all... I ask you in all soberness, if all
these things, if ratified, if confirmed and endorsed, if taught
to our children and repeated to them, do not tend to rub out
the sentiment of liberty in the country, and to transform this
government to some other form?

He pauses momentarily.

                    LINCOLN
This argument of the Judge is the same old serpent that
says, " You work and I eat; you toil and I will enjoy the
fruits of it." Take it whatever way you will, whether it
come from the mouth of a King, an excuse for enslaving
the people of his country, or from the mouth of men of
one race as a reason for enslaving men of another race,
it is all the same old serpent.

He pauses, heading for the climax.

                    LINCOLN
Let us then, turn this government back into the channel
in which the framer's of the Constitution originally
placed it. Let us stand firmly by each other. Let us unite,
as one people throughout the land, until we shall once
more stand up declaring that all men are created equal.
Let us revere the Declaration of Independence; Let us
keep step with the music of the Union; Let us draw a
cordon, so to speak, around the hateful institution, like
a reptile poisoning itself, it will perish by its own infamy.
If we cannot give freedom to every creature, let us do
nothing that will impose slavery on any other creature. We
cannot be free men if this is, by our national choice, to be
a land of slavery. Those who deny freedom to others deserve
it not for themselves; and under the rule of a just God
cannot long retain it. We must make this a land of liberty
in fact as it is in name. Let us have faith that right makes
might, and in that faith, let us, to the end, dare to do our
duty, as we understand it.

THUNDER CRACKS. LIGHTNING FLASHES.

                    LINCOLN
And so on and so forth.

As he steps off the hassock, he stumbles awkwardly.

                    LINCOLN
               (laughing at himself)
Whoa! That'll teach me to get above myself.
               (brushing himself off)
Reminds me of the evening of the day that decided that
Senate contest between Judge Douglas and myself.
It was something like tonight, dark, rainy and gloomy.
The returns being the same, I started for home.

He picks himself up and ambles upstage.

LINCOLN

Now, the path had been worn hog back and was
treacherous.
    (displaying)
My foot slipped from under me knocking the other
one out of the way. For such an awkward fellow, I
am fairly sure footed. It used to take a pretty dexterous
man to throw me.
    (moving down right)
Sangamon County legend has it that I whipped Jack
Armstrong, the leader of the Clary Grove boys, in an
epic wrestling match. I don't know who whipped who,
but I did get their votes when I ran for the State
Legislature….Anyway, I recovered my balance and lit
square and I said to myself, "It's a slip and not a fall."
That thought proved prophetic. Although I lost that
Senate contest, two years later I won the presidency,
defeating Judge Douglas and a split Democratic Party.

He sits on the hassock.

LINCOLN

He's gone now, of course. Passed shortly after the
election. Despite our differences I always considered
him a friend. We had a lot of history together. Oh, there
may have been a bit of jealousy. He courted Mary, you
know, before we tied the knot. Then too it was said that
he tried to paint me as a wealthy aristocrat, Mary being
raised on a plantation. But I don't buy it. Just mischief
makers looking to damage me and win votes. People will
say anything and often do.

He rises and moves upstage to the map.

LINCOLN

Why some have accused Mary of being a traitor simply
because she has relatives fighting on the Confederate
side. When her half sister, Emilie, lost her husband at
Chickamauga, she was barred from returning to her
Kentucky home because she wouldn't swear allegiance
to the Union…I issued a pass and invited her to stay at
the White House for a few days. One of my general's
told me in no uncertain terms that she had to go. I more
or less told him the same. Not that Mary can't speak for
herself. as I think she has proved to all, both North and
South…This was a particularly good thing when we
were courting because I had nothing to say. Well, nothing
of a personal nature. I was fine if we talked politics or
history, but had no feeling for the Drawing Room chit -
chat she was raised on.

TELEGRAPH CHATTER and a TINKLING BELL are heard.

> LINCOLN
> (starting to go)
> One thing's for certain. She's hoping for four more
> years at her current address.

Lincoln exits. Lights dim. CLOCK TICKS. After a brief interval, Lincoln returns with a SHEAF of TELEGRAMS,

> LINCOLN
> Slow but steady returns from Pennsylvania. Well, as
> Pennsylvania goes so goes the nation, or so they say.
> (calling offstage)
> Perhaps someone could tell Mrs. Lincoln! She is more
> anxious than I.
> (pointing at map)
> And let's hope Pennsylvania proves prophetic!

He glances at a telegram then looks up.

> LINCOLN
> There was another Mary in my life, you know, before
> I met Mrs. Lincoln.
> (crossing right)
> A go-between, I mention no names, put it to me that
> Miss Mary Owens of Kentucky would once again return
> to New Salem if I would make the pledge. Even though
> I hadn't seen her for three years, my memory of her was
> favorable, so I agreed. But when we met, I barely
> recognized her. She had gone from pint size to beyond
> plump. It was a drawback but not a deal breaker. I was
> no prize chicken.

He strolls down stage right.

> LINCOLN
> But I worried that she was used to better and I had
> nothing much at all to show on that front. Even though
> I'd begun to practice law, I was saddled with a debt of
> eleven hundred dollars, incurred when a New Salem
> grocery store I took a half share in went to the wall. My
> partner inconveniently passed away, but not his creditors,
> who were very much alive... Although I wasn't legally
> bound to pay his half, I eventually did. But those creditors
> had to be extremely patient. It took me seventeen years to
> clear what I had dubbed my 'National Debt.'.

He places the telegrams on the side table.

LINCOLN

As to the Mary Owens proposal, I feared I could not make
the woman happy and only made a half hearted offer... I
needn't have worried. She let it be known that I was not
the man she pictured as her ideal husband and turned me
down flat. I resolved then and there not ever to marry, as I
could never be satisfied with anyone who would be block-
head enough to have me.

He crosses up right checking his pocket watch.

LINCOLN

By the time I met Mrs. Lincoln I was terrorised by the
thought of the whole enterprise. We had a false step
or two, but after some turmoil, we made the bargain. On
the day of the event someone asked me where I was going.
"To hell, I suppose," I muttered... No family, just the two of
us, a couple of bridesmaids. I vowed to myself to do all in my
power to make her happy. And there was nothing I could
imagine that would make me more unhappy, than to fail
in that attempt. Marriage to me was a profound wonder...
We boarded at the Globe Tavern for four dollars a week.
I went back to my office and Mary bided her time. Even then
she believed that I would some day be president. Whereas
I couldn't imagine such a sucker reaching that high office.

BELL TINKLES offstage.

LINCOLN

Excuse me.

He hurries offstage. The lights dim and CLOCKS TICK. After a brief
interval, Lincoln returns with more TELEGRAMS.

LINCOLN

The night wears on but our patience is being rewarded.
We have heard from Baltimore, a city that has not always
been in our column, especially at the beginning of the
rebellion.
          (moving to the map)
A city whose citizens, you may remember, shot and
killed some of our Massachusetts troops on their
way to defend the Capital, which was under threat of
imminent attack.
          (glancing at telegram)
And now, nearly four years later, Baltimore has come full
circle, giving us a majority of ten thousand, a fair beginning,
and a good omen for taking the entire state of Maryland.
          (glancing at another telegram)
And Massachusetts has given us an 80,000 majority.
Expected, but no less gratifying.

LINCOLN (cont'd)
(smiling)

Tad will be pleased. He's particularly fond of the
Massachusetts Sixth who were the only northern realities
in the District those first days of the war. Fitted him out in
a Union uniform which his mother couldn't get off him.
Now he marches around quite smartly, calls himself the Home
Guard, along with his menagerie of pets I suppose. He's got
a pony, a dog, a kitten, the turkey and a goat. Although
Nannie was exiled after tearing up the lawn at the Soldiers'
Home... Mary thinks I'm too indulgent, allowing him the run
of the place, popping into Cabinet meetings and all. But I
see he misses his brother. I lost my own brother when I was
near his age, and later my sister Sarah in childbirth.... Well,
"there's a divinity that shapes our ends, rough hew them
how we will".
(glancing at another telegram)

Now here's one that got by the boys. "If the ballot does not
remove the despot, we trust some bold hand will pierce his heart
with dagger point for the public good."
(dismissively)

Pigeon hole fodder.

He tosses it on the side table.

LINCOLN

By the way, I don't tell Mrs. Lincoln about these threats,
not since that rumpus at the Soldiers' Home last summer;
no, not Mary's carriage accident. This was another occasion
when out of the blue my horse bolted and ran away with me.
I thought no more about it, but the next day a bullet hole was
found in the crown of the plug hat I'd been wearing;
apparently made by some foolish marksman, not intended
for me. I'll say no more about it.

He sits in the armchair. Rain fills the silence.

LINCOLN

I often come over here to escape my persecutors. Those
long lines of visitors seeking an audience, with their gripes
and grievances. One day when I was especially besieged,
and apparently looking it, I was asked if there was anything
wrong at the Front. "No," I replied, "It isn't the war, it's
post office at Brownsville, Missouri.
(smiling wryly)

That first year it was also death, taxes, currency depreciation,
the National Debt, Mississippi River closed; the war dragging
on disastrous and disgraceful, with no prospect of success.
General McClellan was laid up with typhoid fever and wouldn't
or couldn't reveal his war plans. Chase said he had no money
and told me he could raise no more. The bottom was out of the
tub and all the while the country losing patience....

LINCOLN (cont'd)

Overseas Britain's Cotton Mills were hurting for want of cotton, which caused an unemployment problem for them, especially in Manchester. We had the support of the workers, but their government was threatening to come in on the Confederate side. If they did, France would follow. Something had to be done. I had come to the conclusion that we must free slaves or be ourselves subdued.

He takes a pause.

LINCOLN

I actually wrote the Emancipation Proclamation right here in this room. Quieter here, easier to think. It was my belief that the Constitution invests its Commander in Chief with the laws of war, in the time of war, and according to the laws of war, property, including slaves, could be taken, when needed. The Confederacy was using slaves to build breastworks, trenches, and all manner of war work. It gave them an advantage we couldn't afford. That card had to be taken away from them or there would be no end to the conflict... As a military measure, I would offer slaves in Secessionist States, their freedom..
(after a moment)
Showed a draft of the Proclamation to the Cabinet in late July of '62'. They approved but suggested I wait for a military success before I issued it; that as the war was going so badly, it might be seen as a last shriek, a last desperate gasp to turn things around. So I put it in a drawer and waited for a victory; waited and reflected, like Shakespeare's 'Claudius', on my fears and hopes for the country.

"What if this cursed hand were thicker than itself with brother's blood.
Is there not rain enough in the sweet heaven's
To wash it white as snow....
Help angels, make assay. Bow stubborn knees,
And heart with strings of steel, be soft as sinews
Of the new born babe. All may be well."

He pauses momentarily in thought.

LINCOLN

A Minister once came into my office and told me God was on the side of the Union. I told him I wasn't at all concerned because I knew the Lord was always on the side of right. But that it was my constant anxiety that I and this nation may be on the Lord's side....Quite a different matter.

He rises and moves to the map.

LINCOLN

Two months later, Lee left his base in Virginia and invaded
Pennsylvania. It was unsettling but also an opportunity. His
army was no longer dug in, but exposed.
(referring to map)
General McClellan was shadowing Lee on a parallel line.
Although the general had been relieved of over all
command of the army, he still commanded the Army of
the Potomac, with reservations. Some wanted him
relieved altogether. Cited his failure to aid General Pope
at Bull Run. Felt it was deliberate, and if so, treasonous.
But I felt he had the confidence of the troops, not a minor
factor, so reluctantly left him in command.
(fervently)
Honestly, I would have held the general's horse if he'd
only bring me military success.
(moving behind armchair)
The night before he met Lee's army at Antietam, I went
down on my knees and fervently prayed for a victory; in return
I would issue the Proclamation.... A few days after that battle,
I signed an Executive Order freeing slaves in Secessionist
States, with the intention of making the order permanent in
ninety days. My prayers had been answered – sort of.... The
general's a fine engineer and a good organizer, but when it
comes to the day of battle he gets oppressed by a fear of
failure. He won the day at Antietam and might have shortened
the war if he had pursued Lee's Army.... Two months later he
was relieved, then he resigned, and is currently opposing me
for the presidency, running on a 'peace platform' which
belies his heroic service to the Union cause.
(checking his watch)
Now I have heard it said that there are some who do not want
to win this war. That the strategy is, and has been, to prolong
it until Secessionist States are given favorable terms, independence
and the extension of slavery into new territories and beyond; Cuba
Mexico, South America, possibly swallowing sections of these
countries. If they can't go West, they'll go South. They are that
determined and unrelenting.

TELEGRAPH CHATTER and a TICKLING BELL is heard.

LINCOLN

Which is why this election Is so crucial to the survival of this
government as we know it.

He exits quickly. Light dim. CLOCK TICKS..

"Watching with Lincoln"

Part Three

Lincoln returns with TELEGRAMS.

LINCOLN
(studying telegram breathlessly)
New York predicts a 40,000 majority for McClellan....
If it holds, if it is not reversed, I may win the election
but lose the nation. Pressure for an armistice would
grow. Once agreed, the country could never go back
to war. It wouldn't be feasible. It would mean, in effect,
the immediate dissolution of the Union.

He paces thoughtfully in front of the map.)

LINCOLN
No doubt the Proclamation has been a two edged sword
and that is reflected in the voting. No doubt some felt,
and still feel, it did not go far enough. They wanted all
the slaves freed, not just slaves in Secessionist States....
Others demanded universal suffrage. But that might have
caused us to lose support in Border States like Kentucky
and Missouri that were still with us... I did favor suffrage
for black men who fought, and to that end we encouraged
former slaves to enlist, which they did. And that too was
a problem for some. They didn't mind fighting to save the
Union, but didn't want to fight to free the slaves.
(crossing down left center)
To those who say they will not fight to free the Negro, I
say fight then exclusively to save the Union. But when
peace comes, there will be some black men who can remember
that with silent tongue and clenched teeth, and steady eye,
and well poised bayonet, they have helped mankind on to
this mighty consummation. While I fear there will be some
white ones unable to forget, that with malignant heart,
and deceitful speech, they have strove to hinder it.
(moving stage right)
My paramount object in this struggle is to save the Union,
and not either to save or destroy slavery. If I could save the
Union without freeing slaves, I would have done it. And if
I could save it by freeing all the slaves, I would have done
it. And if I could save it by freeing some and leaving others
alone, I would also have done that. What I now do about
slavery, I do because it helps to save the Union. And what I
forbear, I forbear, because I do not believe it would help
to save the Union. And that is why I issued the Emancipation
Proclamation...

He sits in the armchair.

LINCOLN

I signed it on New Year's Day, a day we traditionally have a
reception at the White House. I didn't want history thinking
there was any hesitancy or reluctance on my part when I
signed that document. So despite my sore hand, sore from
all the hand shaking, I made certain my signature was sure and
steady. There could be no turning back... I will not retract or
modify the Proclamation, nor will I return to slavery any person
who is free by that Proclamation...To safeguard any legal
challenge, an amendment to the Constitution must be passed
by Congress and ratified by Union States and some of the
Reconstructed States. Ratification will hasten the end of the war,
which was my dearest hope.
(glancing at a telegram)
But if New York and New Jersey both go down, which is now
predicted, the Emancipation Proclamation, the Union, and
this brief experiment in a people's government could be -
no more.
(glancing at another telegram)
From Grant. "The election, having come off quietly is a victory
worth more to the country than a battle won."... Some thought
the general might oppose me for the presidency. His military
record would have made him a formidable candidate. Fortunately
for the country, he let it be known that his only interest was in
the defeat of the Confederacy and the restoration of the Union.
Certainly he has shown himself to be true to that aspiration...
His successes at Fort Donelson and Shiloh in the early months
of the war were a beacon of hope where none could be found.
Yes, I know his troops suffered heavy losses, especially at Shiloh,
and for this he was castigated as a butcher and a drunk, many
wanted him relieved. I suggested they find out the general's
brand of whiskey and give it to my other generals. I couldn't
spare the man. He fights. His victory at Vicksburg after delays
and set backs, was ingenious and stunning and seemed to put the
rebellion on the back foot.

He rises vigorously and goes to the map.

LINCOLN

Especially as it coincided with Meade's victory at Gettysburg.
Both victories, occurring on the fourth of July, seemed
almost mystical, and roused the country to hope for a quick
end to the conflict.
(pointing to the map)
Vicksburg opened up the Mississippi valley. Gettysburg
put Lee's army on the defensive. But in one case, enemy
soldiers were paroled and in the other – allowed to slip
away.

LINCOLN (cont'd)
.   (quickly)
Don't misunderstand me about General Meade. I am
profoundly grateful, down to my boots, for what he did
at Gettysburg. But I think if I had been the general, I would
have fought one more battle. He held the war in his hands
and did not close it...and so it continues.
(edging down enter)
It was increasingly apparent to me that I was not in control
of events... but that events controlled me.

He moves behind the armchair.

LINCOLN
On the day of Meade's victory, Serenaders came to the White
House. In my brief remarks a theme began which reached
full fruition four months later at the memorial service
for all those who fell on that battlefield.

A flute softly plays "Abide with Me".

LINCOLN
The day prior to the service, Tad came down with a high
fever. Since Willie died, Mary was easily frightened and
urged me to stay. I was concerned but felt I had to go. The
occasion was too important, thousands would be attending.
(crossing D.S.C.)
The Minister gave a lengthy invocation that was probably
longer than my address. Then for two hours, Edward Everett
spoke movingly of the battle itself. After another hymn, it
was my turn.

He steps on the hassock. Lights dim around him.

LINCOLN
"Four score and seven years ago, our fathers brought forth
upon this continent, a new nation, conceived in liberty and
dedicated to the proposition - that all men are created equal.

Now we are engaged in a great civil war, testing whether
that nation or any nation, so conceived and so dedicated
can long endure.

We are met on a great battlefield of that war. We have
come to dedicate a portion of that field as a final
resting place for those, who here, gave their lives that
nation might live... It is altogether fitting and proper
that we should do this.

LINCOLN (cont'd)

But in a larger sense, we cannot dedicate, we cannot
consecrate, we cannot hallow this ground. The brave men,
living and dead, who struggled here, have consecrated it
far above our power to add or detract. The world will little
note nor long remember what we say here. But it can
never forget what they – did here.

It is for us, the living rather, to be dedicated here to the
unfinished work, which they who fought here, have thus
far, so nobly advanced. It is rather for us to be here
dedicated to the great task remaining before us. That
from these honored dead, we take increased devotion to
that cause for which they gave the last full measure of
devotion.

That we here highly resolve that these dead shall not have
died in vain. That this nation, under God, shall have a new
birth of freedom. And that government of the people, by
the people and for the people, shall not perish from the earth."

Lights gradually come up around him.

LINCOLN

I felt the speech was a flat failure.... I didn't mind so much
for myself, but some of those people came an awful long way.
Press reaction was mixed, both praise and blame.
            (stepping off hassock)
Some of the latter raged that the speech had broadened the
aims of the war from Union to Equality and Union....
            (sitting in armchair)
I can't refute that. To me the two are inseparable.
            (slight pause)
So many have fallen. Not just at Gettysburg... Twice at
Bull Run in the early days. Fredricksburg, Chancellorville...
the Wilderness campaign, Spotsylvania, Petersburg,
and so on and so forth...the South as well with proportional
losses. "My God, my God," I thought. "What will the country
say? What will the country say?"... I looked to Shakespeare.
King John seemed to fit.

            "The sun's o'er cast with blood, fair day
            adieu.
            Which is the side that I must go withal?
            I am with both, each army hath a hand,
            And in their rage, I having hold of both,
            They whirl asunder and dismember me."

The WIND HOWLS, rattling the window.

LINCOLN

When Confederate troops invaded Maryland and
Pennsylvania a few months ago, the Capital was threatened.
Some wanted to evacuate the city.

He rises quickly and heads for the map.

LINCOLN

I got so mad, I rode over to Fort Stevens, which was being
shelled by the Confederates, stood on the parapet and
faced the fire. I wanted the troops to see me there.
(after a moment)
Eventually I was persuaded to duck. I guess I would have
been quite a prize at that.

He pauses, listening to the wind.

LINCOLN

I had a dream the other night which has haunted me
ever since. I had been up waiting for important
dispatches from the Front. I could not have been asleep
long before I began to dream... Then I heard people
weeping. I thought I left my bed and wandered downstairs. I
went from room to room meeting the same mournful sounds
of distress. I was puzzled and alarmed... I continued on until
I arrived in the East Room... Before me was a catafalque on
which rested a corpse. Around it were stationed soldiers and
there was a throng of people. "Who is dead in the White
House?" I demanded of one of the soldiers. "The president",
he said. "He was killed by an assassin."
(quoting Byron)

"Sleep has its own world.
A boundary between the things misnamed
Death and existence. Sleep has its own world,
And a wide realm of wild reality."

He chuckles, then smiles ruefully.

LINCOLN

Reminds me of the old farmer in Illinois whose family
was made sick from eating greens. He said, "Afore we
eat these greens, let's try 'em on Jake," his bear fighting
boy. "If he stands 'em, we're alright." Just so with me.
If the imaginary assassin continues to exercise himself on
others, I can stand it. Anyway, I'll say no more about it.
It wasn't me but some other fellow.

He turns upstage left, but quickly turns back.

LINCOLN

Don't mention that dream to Mary. She's anxious enough
without pouring fuel on the fire. Her nerves seem to be
always on edge. She lost her mother, you know, when she
was very young, about the same age as me when my mother
passed. But I was fortunate in that my stepmother, Sarah
Bush Johnston, was someone who brought light and joy into
the house, was never partial to her own three children
above my sister Sarah and myself.

TELEGRAPH CHATTER is heard offstage.

LINCOLN

Mary, on the other hand, never had the sense that she was
appreciated, never out grew it, and so looks to others for
approval of her worth. Now she's buying a lot of expensive
jewellery, and what not, because she feels judged.

BELL TINKLES LOUDLY.

LINCOLN

I know she is not popular in some quarters. But I
forbear it. Because I know she is worthy.

Lincoln exits. Lights dim. CLOCK TICKS. After a brief interval, Lincoln
returns with more TELEGRAMS.

LINCOLN

New York has been reversed!!!
                (reading)
The prediction is now for a 35,000 majority in the city
and 40,000 in the state…. Well, that's reassuring.
Those earlier numbers for McClellan did seem wide of
the mark. Let's hope it holds.
                (sifting telegrams)
Michigan, Wisconsin and Ohio look to be going our way.
That should offset losses in Kentucky, New Jersey and
Delaware. Nothing yet from Illinois, but if things continue
as they are…
                (laying telegrams on side table)
By the way, the boys in the Telegraph Room have sent out
for some oysters to keep everyone going. I'm not sure if I
can manage oysters at this late hour…
                (checking his watch)
Well after three… But you're welcome.
                (moving to map)
I'll tell you if Illinois goes south, I'll be sorry I didn't get
back there to vote. I have a lot of history there.

He takes a step or two down stage.

LINCOLN

We came to Decatur, Illinois from Pigeon Creek, Indiana
in 1830. I sold notions along the way and made a profit. I
was always looking for a way to profit somehow or other.
A year or so later, Denton Offut came up from New
Salem and asked my cousin, John Hanks, to establish
a boat enterprise taking goods to New Orleans. That
was in March of '31'.

He strolls closer to the 'Watchers".

LINCOLN

John and I came down the Sangamon River in a canoe,
where a mill dam owned by, Mister James Rutledge,
stopped our progress.
(sitting on the hassock)
Mr. Rutledge had founded the town of New Salem a
couple of years prior to our arrival. Anyway, after we built
a flat boat and delivered our goods to the market in
New Orleans, Offut offered me a job working in his New
Salem grocery store. That's how I came to settle there.
That's how I got to know Anne Rutledge. After a time we
came to an understanding, but … it was not to be. She got
the fever and passed. ..That event set me back on my heels.
It was so bad I couldn't bear the thought of rain falling on
her grave. I truly loved the girl and think often of her now.
…I plundered Burns for comfort.

"Oh thou pale orb that silent shines,
Where care untroubled mortals sleep,
Thou seest a wretch that inly pines,
And wanders here to wail and weep.
With woe I nightly vigils keep,
Beneath thy wan unwarming beam,
And mourn in lamentation deep,
How life and love are all a dream."

Folks in New Salem were concerned about me. Got me
a job as their postmaster. And then an opportunity to
do some surveying sprang up. I studied Euclid and did
that for a time, laid out a few towns thereabouts with
my two chain men. Something always seemed to go my way.
I've always been grateful to the folks of New Salem.
Every man is said to have his peculiar ambition.
Whether it be true or not, I can say, for one, that I
had no other so great as that of being truly esteemed of
my fellow men by rendering myself worthy of their esteem.

BELL TINKLES offstage.

                         LINCOLN
        Excuse me.

Lincoln exits, then returns quickly, munching away.

                         LINCOLN
        Oysters! Just one to show my appreciation.
                (wiping mouth with handkerchief)
        I am forced to confess that I am relieved of suspense
        and am glad that the verdict of the people –
                (pointing at the map)
        - including a 20,000 majority from Illinois, is so
        likely to be clear, full and unmistakable!!!

The faint strains of a BAND STRIKING UP can be heard in the distance.

                         LINCOLN
        I'd go home and give Mary the news, but that Band
        must have roused her. She's probably up making
        plans. We might be roused ourselves if we cracked open
        a couple of those windows.

He crosses up to the coat tree, retrieves his hat, and 'notes' hidden in the lining.

                         LINCOLN
        I had thought of returning to my law practice in Illinois
        if things hadn't gone my way. The law for me will
        always hold a fascination.
                (studying notes)
        I love to dig up a legal question by the roots, and hold it
        up, and dry it before the fires of the mind.... Sometimes
        I'd study legal precedents stretching back to English
        Common Law. This was partly self interest.
                (crossing down left)
        I didn't dare trust a case on the preconception that the
        Court knows all things. I argued on the preconception
        that the Court doesn't know anything at all.

He chuckles and glances at his notes.

                         LINCOLN
        I prepared a few notes... just in case...
                (looking up)
        My law partner was always trying to get me to talk
        faster. But the long convolutions of my brain won't
        allow for such an approach. I have to talk slowly.

He rears back like a runner about to race.

LINCOLN
I commence way back like the boys do when they want
to get a good start. My weight and speed give me
momentum to jump far. I think I'll jump to Europe
when my work is done here. And then to the West.
I want to see the Rockies, California, the rest of the
country.

BAND MUSIC CLIMAXES.

LINCOLN
(stepping on hassock)
I guess I'll risk the hassock.

WILD CHEERS from the CROWD.

LINCOLN
Thank you. Thank you all.
(pocketing his notes)
The present rebellion brought our Republic to a
severe test. And a presidential election occurring in
regular course during the rebellion, added not a little
to the strain. But the election was a necessity. And
now that the election is over, may not all, having a
common interest, reunite in a common effort, to save
our common country. For my part I have striven and
will continue to strive to avoid placing any obstacle
in the way. So long as I have been here I have not
willingly planted a thorn in any man's bosom.... While
I am deeply sensible to the high compliment of re-
election and duly grateful, it adds nothing to my
satisfaction that any other man may be disappointed
or pained by the result.

Slight pause.

LINCOLN
May I ask those of you who have not differed with me,
to join with me in the same spirit towards those who
have... With malice toward none, with charity toward
all, with firmness in the right as God gives us to see
the right, let us strive to finish the work we are in, to
bind up the nation's wounds, to care for him who shall
have borne the battle, and his widow and his orphan.
To do all that may achieve and cherish a just and lasting
peace among ourselves and with all nations... Surely
God intends some great good to follow this mighty
convulsion, which no mortal could make and no mortal
could stay....Now - will you do me a favor? Would you
play one of my favorite tunes? Will you play "Dixie"?

The BAND plays a ROUSING "DIXIE". The CROWD ROARS its approval.

LINCOLN

Splendid! And now it is late. And with the dawn we
have work to do. Thank you for coming. Goodnight,
and God bless.

Lincoln steps off the hassock to a ROAR of APPLAUSE.

LINCOLN
(glancing at his notes)

Well - I'll work on it.

He crosses to the coat tree and slips his notes back into the seam of his hat.
In the b.g. we hear the BAND and the MUSIC receding .

LINCOLN

And to those of you who have watched with me into
the wee small hours – a special thanks. I hope I
have not kept you from your sleep – too long.
(raising his hat)
Enjoy the oysters!

FREEZE ON LINCOLN

Lights fade to black.

THE END

.

.

SENECA FALLS FOREVER

A Play

By

Michael J Shannon

U.S. Copyright
Pau 4-136-097
Completion April, 2022

Author's Note

'Seneca Falls Forever" is my latest play, chronologically speaking. However, it is thematically a close relative to my earlier plays, "Watching with Lincoln" , "JFK on JFK" and "Liberty Rising", all of which touch on the progression of human rights and the equality of man. In this case it is women's rights that is the focus, and their battle to be recognized as fully fledged citizens.

The play begins in the spring of 1917, on the night in which President Wilson announced America's entrance into the First World War. Ironically, that war significantly propelled the cause of women's suffrage and led to the passage of the 19th amendment a few years later. The play celebrates that journey.

"SENECA FALLS FOREVER"

The Gordon family home, Seneca Falls,
New York. Dining Room.

Time: April 2, 1917, Evening.

A BIRTHDAY CAKE with a few
candles is being carried by GWEN
PIERCE GORDON, late 30's, into the
dimly lit dining room, while a chorus
of VOICES sings 'HAPPY BIRTHDAY'.

> VOICES
"Happy Birthday to you, Happy Birthday
to you. Happy Birthday Grandma Letty,
Happy Birthday to you!!!"

Everyone CHEERS and CLAPS as Gwen places the cake
in front of her mother, GRANDMA LETTY.

With no hesitation, Grandma Letty blows out the candles.
More CHEERING and CLAPPING.

RUSSELL GORDON, mid 40's, sits at the head of the table.)

> RUSSELL
John, give us some light, would you?

JOHN GORDON, eighteen, rises quickly and snaps on
the overhead light.

> GWEN
> (to Grandma Letty)
Did you make a wish?

> GRANDMA LETTY
Yes.

Seventeen year old, ALICE GORDON, chimes in.

> ALICE
What did you wish for?

> GRANDMA LETTY
Another birthday.

Everyone laughs.

                    RUSSELL
I think that's what we're all wishing for
this evening.

HAL NEWBURY, Alice's eighteen year old 'beau',
pipes up.

                    HAL
I'll say.

                    GWEN
Russell, you promised.

                    RUSSELL
I said nothing.

                    JOHN
Do you really think it'll come to war, dad?

                    GWEN
John!

                    RUSSELL
It wouldn't surprise me.

                    GWEN
Alice, would you hand me those dessert
plates on the sideboard?

Alice rises to get the plates.

                    RUSSELL
The president's addressing Congress as
we sit here tonight enjoying this delicious
cake. He didn't call them into session to
discuss the weather.

Gwen takes the cake to her chair and sits.

                    GWEN
I voted for President Wilson because he
promised to keep us out of war, and so
did you.

                    RUSSELL
I know, dear, but –

                    GWEN
Who wants cake?

                    RUSSELL
It seems to me the president's between a
rock and a hard place.

                    GWEN
Mother?

                GRANDMA LETTY
No.

                    GWEN
Of course you do.

                    RUSSELL
He doesn't want to go to war, but he's
been given no choice.

                    GWEN
Pass this down to mother, would you,
John?

                    RUSSELL
Their U-Boats are sinking our Merchant
Fleet again, despite our declared neutrality.

                    GWEN
Sophie?

                    SOPHIE
Not too big a slice. I have to watch my
figure.

SOPHIE EMERSON is John's eighteen year old girl friend.

                    HAL
Don't worry, Soph. John's watching it
for you.

He chuckles. Sophie blushes. Alice is outraged on
Sophie's behalf.

                    ALICE
Hal!

                    HAL
Just kidding.

RUSSELL
And now it seems their government is
plotting with Mexico to start a war
with us.

ALICE
Sophie is John's guest.

HAL
Sorry, Sophie.

SOPHIE
(taking the cake)
That's alright.

RUSSELL
Promising to give them Texas, New
Mexico and Arizona if they'll go along
with the scheme. The country's incensed.

GWEN
Hal?

HAL
You bet.

ALICE
Not that he deserves any.

JOHN
Oh, come on, Alice.

GWEN
Pass that to Hal, would you Alice?

RUSSELL
There's also been talk of Japan getting
involved in the plot.

GWEN
Japan? Whatever for? Aren't they with
the Allies?

RUSSELL
Indeed they are.

GWEN
Alice?

                    ALICE
No thanks.

                    RUSSELL
All the more reason for the other side to
distract them with false promises of rich
pickings.

                    GWEN
John?

                    JOHN
                 (to Gwen)
You bet.

                    RUSSELL
Of course, now that the cat's out of the bag,
the scheme probably won't come to
anything.

Gwen passes John a slice.

                    GWEN
Russell?

                    RUSSELL
What?

                    GWEN
Cake?

                    RUSSELL
Certainly. I stopped watching my figure
year's ago.

Everyone laughs. Gwen passes him a slice.

                    RUSSELL
Anyway, it's a darn shame.

                    GWEN
What is?

                    RUSSELL
That the president's been trying to broker an
even handed peace deal for months. "Peace
without Victory". "Peace among Equals." And
now, with this latest calamity, he feels betrayed,
and the country along with him.

Pause.

                    ALICE
How old are you now Grandma?

                    GRANDMA LETTY
No idea.

                    JOHN
She was born before the civil war.

                    GRANDMA LETTY
Says who?

                    JOHN
You. You told me.

                    GRANDMA LETTY
I did?

                    JOHN
Yes. And that your father was an officer
in the Union Army.

                    GRANDMA LETTY
I really don't remember...he died you know.

Slight pause.

                    RUSSELL
By the way, I noticed the wind blew down
that "VOTES FOR WOMEN" sign on the
front lawn again.

                    GWEN
Oh, no. That's the third time this month.

                    JOHN
Maybe we should wire it to the porch.

                    ALICE
I suspect sabotage.

                    GWEN
Sabotage? Don't be silly.

                    RUSSELL
By who?

GWEN
Never mind.

ALICE
One of the neighbors?

GWEN
In Seneca Falls?

ALICE
Not necessarily one of our neighbors.

GWEN
I should hope not.

JOHN
Outside agitators?

ALICE
Could be.

GWEN
I don't believe it.

RUSSELL
Well, Seneca Falls is where it all started,
as you so often remind me. Could be a
symbolic gesture from the antis.

HAL
Really?

RUSSELL
Oh, yes. 1848. 300 met to discuss women's
rights at the Wesleyan Chapel, not far from
here.

ALICE
Grandma Letty's mother was there, wasn't
she grandma?

GRANDMA LETTY
Where?

ALICE
At the Wesleyan Chapel in 1848.

GRANDMA LETTY

If you say so..

ALICE

Mama says so.

GRANDMA LETTY

Well, if she says so, it must be true. I've
always known your mother to be truthful.

RUSSELL

Quakers, weren't they?

GWEN

Who?

RUSSELL

At the Chapel.

JOHN

We could lay a camera trap for the saboteurs.

GWEN

I believe so, at least the organizers. Anyone for seconds?

SOPHIE

Is that why you're so keen on women's
rights, Mrs. Gordon? Because of your great
grandmother?

GWEN

No. We never met.

RUSSELL

I'll indulge, if no one else cares to.

JOHN
(to Hal)
My mother belongs to a group who think
women should be allowed to vote.

ALICE

NAWASA.

HAL

Really?

GWEN

Carrie Catt's group.

ALICE

She's famous.

RUSSELL
(taking cake)
You'll soon learn, Hal, that in this house
women's suffrage is a hot topic.

HAL

Hotter even than the war?

GWEN

There is no war. And if the president is
half the man I think he is, there won't be
one.

RUSSELL

We'll know soon enough. A few of the
town fathers are waiting at the telegraph
office for news. I asked them to call me.

JOHN

How about you, grandma? Do you think
women should be allowed to vote?

Grandma Letty concentrates on her cake.

GWEN

Mother?

GRANDMA LETTY

What?

GWEN

John asked you a question.

GRANMA LETTY

I'm indifferent.

GWEN

Oh, mother, you're not.

GRANDMA LETTY

I don't believe in picketing the White
House and causing a ruckus, or going to jail,
I'll tell you that.

GWEN

That's Alice Paul's group, not mine. But I do
understand their frustration and admire
their grit.

GRANDMA LETTY

It's true my mother was for suffrage…
dragged me along with her when I was
about twelve or thirteen. Met Cady Stanton
in Rochester I believe it was…no longer with
us – and no wonder. Worn out from all that
campaigning.

RUSSELL
(chuckling)
No more cake for grandma.

HAL

How about you, Alice?

GWEN

Alice is with us. Always helps me with
petitions and signs and a hundred other
things.

ALICE
(sighing)
I'll say.

GWEN

You may groan, but you'll get the benefit
if New York passes the referendum this
Fall.

SOPHIE

Didn't we just have a referendum?

RUSSELL

Two years ago. Lost by 100,000 votes.

GWEN

Which is why we can't let up. It's war.

The phone RINGS. Russell rises.

RUSSELL

Speaking of which –

He goes. Slight pause.

> ALICE
> All finished, grandma?

> GRANDMA LETTY
> Yes, all done.

> ALICE
> You belong to the 'clean your plate club',
> grandma. Not a crumb left.

> GWEN
> She certainly does.

> JOHN
> Well done, grandma.

> ALICE
> A toast to Grandma Letty.

> ALL
> (toasting)
> To Grandma Letty!

Cheers, as Russell returns and takes his seat. All
eyes turn to him.

> GWEN
> Well?

> RUSSELL
> As I suspected - the president has asked
> Congress for a Declaration of War.

Pause.

> GWEN
> Would you like a cup of tea, mother?

> GRANDMA LETTY
> No.

> GWEN
> You're sure?

She nods.

GWEN

Okay. Give me two minutes to tidy up,
then we'll go into the parlor and open
presents. Won't that be nice. Russell, help
mother into the parlor, would you?

Russell steals a last mouthful of cake, then rises.

GWEN

Alice, could you clear the plates.

Alice rises and begins collecting plates.

HAL

I'll help.

Hal, with Alice, collects plates, while Russell
escorts grandma Letty to the parlor.

GWEN

Perhaps some music, Russell. One of
mother's favorites.

Alice and Hal disappear, Gwen, near tears, steals
a glance at John.

GWEN
(calling)
Never mind, Russell, I'll do it.

Gwen hurries after Russell.

GWEN

I know what she likes.

Lights fade to black. "Moonlight Bay" plays softly.

ACT 1

Scene 2

Front Porch

Moments later.

Lights fade up on John and Sophie sitting on a small wicker love seat.

The music from the gramophone continues in the b.g.

Occasionally, we hear Ooh's and Ahs from the parlor as presents are opened by grandma Letty.

> SOPHIE
> Maybe we should go in.

> JOHN
> What for?

> SOPHIE
> I don't want to offend your grandmother.

> JOHN
> We won't be missed.

> SOPHIE
> You're sure?

> JOHN
> Yes.

> SOPHIE
> I'm just thinking of you. She doesn't know
> me from Adam.

> JOHN
> She will. I mean... I hope she will.

Pause.

> SOPHIE
> I just can't believe it. Can you?

> JOHN
> No ... it's a shock.

SOPHIE
I thought the president was dead set against
going to war.

JOHN
Everybody did.

SOPHIE
I know they're sinking our ships, but that's been
going on from the beginning, hasn't it?

JOHN
It has, yes.

SOPHIE
I remember when they sank the Lusitania. All
those people.

JOHN
Yeah. That was pretty grim. But then I didn't
hear much.

SOPHIE
Me either. Not that I've been following the
reports too closely.

JOHN
Who has? I don't think you can fault yourself
on that score, Sophie.

SOPHIE
It's just so unbelievable.

JOHN
I know.

SOPHIE
Do you think there's any chance Congress
won't go along?

Laughter from the parlor is heard.

JOHN
Hardly any...not since that plot to drag us
into a war with Mexico was uncovered.

SOPHIE
And Japan too your father said.

JOHN
Maybe. I'm not too sure about the details.

Pause.

SOPHIE
What will you do?

JOHN
About what?

SOPHIE
If it's war...

JOHN
Haven't really thought...

SOPHIE
No, how could you.

They are silent for a moment, listening to the music from the parlor.

JOHN
Wanna dance?

SOPHIE
No.

JOHN
How come?

SOPHIE
They'll see us.

JOHN
Let them.

SOPHIE
I'd be embarrassed.

JOHN
Come on.

SOPHIE
You're crazy.

JOHN
Pretty soon I might be doing crazier
things than dancing on the front porch.

SOPHIE
Well... maybe – around the side.

He takes her hand. They rise and begin to dance.

SOPHIE
Isn't it a beautiful night.

JOHN
Not too cold?

SOPHIE
No... well, a little.

He holds her closer.

JOHN
There .... now we can keep each other
warm.

SOPHIE
John.

JOHN
Yes.

SOPHIE
What was the first thing you thought
when you heard the news?

JOHN
I don't know.

SOPHIE
I confess – I was a little excited, and
horrified all at the same time.

JOHN
Well –

SOPHIE
Do you think I'm terrible?

JOHN
No, I could never think that.

SOPHIE
What about you? Tell the truth.

JOHN
Okay. My first thought was there goes
my last season of baseball at Seneca Falls
High... pretty selfish, huh.

SOPHIE
No, not really. I know how much you love
baseball.

Laughter and ooh's from the parlour. They dance
toward the side porch.

SOPHIE
Look at all those stars.

JOHN
Yeah, they're all out.

SOPHIE
Makes me feel like we'll live forever.

As they disappear we hear Alice calling.

ALICE (offstage)
John! ... Sophie!

Alice comes out on the porch and looks around.

ALICE
(to herself)
Now, where did they get to?

Hal comes out behind her.

ALICE
John!

No answer.

HAL
Maybe they went for a walk.

                    ALICE
I wouldn't be surprised. Just like John to
leave me to open presents with mother
and dad and Grandma Letty while he goes
strolling with Sophie.

                    HAL
You can't really blame him, wanting to be
alone with his girl friend.

                    ALICE
No, I suppose not.

                    HAL
Anyway, I don't think your grandma noticed.

                    ALICE
It was very kind of you to give her those
handkerchiefs.

                    HAL
All I could think of.

                    ALICE
She seemed pleased.

                    HAL
I did it for you. I didn't want you to think I
was a dead beat. Show up at a birthday party
with no present. . .

                    ALICE
Goodness, what a beautiful night.

                    HAL
Care to sit down?

                    ALICE
I'd love to, but I really should get back.

                    HAL
Just for a minute.

                    ALICE
                (glancing back)
Well, okay. Just for a minute.

They sit. Slight pause.

HAL

Your grandmother's quite a live wire.

ALICE

You think so?

HAL

Very up to date with the women's vote,
at least.

ALICE

Oh, that's mother. She gives her all the news.

HAL

I'll bet. She's seems pretty fierce – your
mother.

ALICE

Oh, no, not really. It's all this talk of war.
Normally, she's a peach.

HAL

Yeah. It's – hard to believe.

ALICE

Yes.

HAL

Your brother seems to be taking it
well enough.

ALICE

Oh, that's just his way.

HAL

Still waters, eh.

ALICE

Or something.

HAL

Me. I'm more up front. What you see is
what you get.

ALICE

I like what I see.

HAL

Really?

ALICE

I can't believe I said that. It must be the
news.

HAL

I never thought I'd be grateful to –

ALICE

Don't say that. I hate war.

HAL

So do I.

ALICE

What will you do, Hal?

HAL

I'm not volunteering, I'll tell you that.
If I go, they'll have to come and get me.
I'm not like your brother.

ALICE

What about my brother?

HAL

Nothing.

ALICE

Please.

HAL

Well, we were asking each other what
we'd do, you know, if it came to it. And
John said he wouldn't wait for the draft –
that he'd volunteer.

ALICE

Oh.

HAL

He never said?

ALICE

No.

HAL

I tell you my dad'id kill me if I joined up.
Thinks it's all a sucker's game.

ALICE
Is that what you think?

HAL
I don't know what the hell I think,
pardon my French. It's hard for me to
go against my dad...and then there's
you I have to think about. I haven't
told you, but now with things being as
they are... you should know I'm awfully
fond of you, Alice.

ALICE
I'm fond of you too, Hal, in a best friend
kind of way.

HAL
I'm glad to hear it, Alice, and if it wasn't
for this darn war, I wouldn't put you on
the spot. I don't mean to rush things, but –

ALICE
Of course not. I see that. I – well – I'm so -
inexperienced... all my thoughts – I'm still
in high school, and then there's college to be
considered, and now even those plans may go
out the window...who knows what will happen.
Everything seems to be at sixes and sevens.
With you as well. I'm sure you're just as
confused.

HAL
I am. You're the one thing I'm not confused
about.

GWEN (offstage)
(calling)
Alice!...

ALICE
Would you like to go for a walk? Maybe
we'll run into John and Sophie.

HAL
Sure.

GWEN (offstage)
Alice! Are you out there?

They go off together just as Gwen comes out on the porch.

>GWEN
>(calling)
>Alice! ... John!

Russell appears behind her.

>GWEN
>Now where did they get to?

>RUSSELL
>I'm sure all is well.

>GWEN
>If only that were true. Did mother get to
>bed alright?

>RUSSELL
>Yes, happy as a clam. Took the stairs two
>at a time .... lovely night.

>GWEN
>Is it?

>RUSSELL
>Don't take my word for it. Take a deep
>breath. Fix you right up. Better than castor
>oil...

Slight pause.

>RUSSELL
>It was kind of Hal to bring a present for
>your mother.

>GWEN
>He knows he'll get brownie points with
>Alice.

>RUSSELL
>Didn't you like him?

>GWEN
>After that phone call, I hardly noticed him.

>RUSSELL
>I think he's smitten.

GWEN

She's too young.

RUSSELL

Yes, I know, but what can you do. I married
you at eighteen.

He slips an arm around her.

GWEN
(calling louder)
John! ... Alice!

No answer.

GWEN

Oh, what's to become of us, Russell?

Music from the parlor ends. Lights fade to black.

ACT 1

Scene 3

Parlor, Gordon Home

Time: Late September, 1917

Grandma Letty sits in a winged
backed chair, knitting.

Gwen can be heard talking on the phone.

GWEN (on phone)
I'm sorry, Hattie, but things have been –
of course we have to get out the vote. I'm
well aware of that... not today, no. My son,
John, is leaving for Camp Upton this afternoon.
it's not that kind of camp. It's an army
camp....Long Island, New York...exciting in
a way, yes, but – more anxious than proud,
I'd say....Of course, he'll be alright. Why
shouldn't he be?

JOHN (offstage)
Mother!

GWEN (on phone)
Anyway, thank you for your concern. Let's
speak tomorrow.

JOHN (offstage)
Mother! Have you seen my blue sweat shirt?

GWEN
(calling)
No! Where did you leave it?

Gwen enters dabbing her eyes with a handkerchief.

JOHN (offstage)
In the laundry basket!

John appears. Gwen pockets the handkerchief.

GWEN
Oh, for goodness sake!
(crossing off)
It's too late now. It'll never be dry in time.

JOHN
That's okay. I probably won't wear it.

A KNOCK is heard at the door.

GWEN (offstage)
Now, who could that be?

GRANDMA LETTY
All packed?

JOHN
Getting there.

GWEN (offstage)
Oh, Hal!. Alice is passing out "Liberty Bond" fliers at the Mill, but John's in the parlor. Please come in.

HAL (offstage)
Thanks.

We hear the door close. Hal enters.

JOHN
Hal!

HAL
Yeah.

JOHN
I can't believe it. I thought you were in Indiana stoking at the steel mills.

HAL
I was – for awhile, but the Unions are tough. Hard to get past the front gate unless you've got experience or some pull... anyway, I heard from Alice that you were leaving for Upton and so I thought I'd –

JOHN
Glad you did.
          (noticing grandma)
Hi there.

GRANDMA LETTY
Hello.

                    JOHN
        Grandma, you remember Hal Newbury?

She stares.

                     HAL
        What are you knitting?

                GRANDMA LETTY
        Socks.

                     HAL
        Oh.

                GRANDMA LETTY
        For John. He's going camping somewhere
        or other.

Phone RINGS offstage.

                    JOHN
        Long Island.

                GRANDMA LETTY
        That's it. Winter's coming so he'll need
        to keep his feet warm.

                GWEN (offstage)
        John! Phone!

                    JOHN
             (calling)
        Who is it?

                GWEN (offstage)
        No idea!

                    JOHN
        Excuse me.

John goes

                GRANDMA LETTY
        I remember you now. You gave me those
        nice handkerchiefs for my birthday.

                     HAL
        That's it.

                    GRANDMA LETTY
    Are you going camping with John?

                    HAL
    No, not today. Maybe later.

                    RANDMA LETTY
    I'd be happy to knit you a pair of
    socks when you do.

                    HAL
    Swell. That'd be great.

                    GRANDMA LETTY
    Just let me know.

                    HAL
    Okay.

                    GRANDMA LETTY
    When do you think that might be?

                    HAL
    Not sure. Pretty soon, I guess.

                    GRANDMA LETTY
    Then I better get started. What color
    would you like?

John returns.

                    JOHN
    Sorry about that. Seems the phone
    never stops ringing.

                    HAL
    Big day.

                    JOHN
    I guess.

                    HAL
    I was just telling your grandmother
    I might be following in your footsteps.

                    JOHN
    You've heard from Uncle Sam?

                    HAL
I'm on the list for the next batch of
of call ups. November/December.

                    JOHN
What about the exemption?

                    HAL
That was a pipe dream.

                    JOHN
Well – golly.

                    HAL
Not a problem. Grandma Letty's promised
me a pair of socks, haven't you?

                    GRANDMA LETTY
Oh, yes.

                    JOHN
Well then – you're all set.

Gwen appears.

                    GWEN
Your blue sweat shirt has been hand
washed and is hanging on the line.
But I'm not sure it'll be dry enough to
pack. You might have to hand carry it.

                    JOHN
Oh, gee, thanks.

                    GWEN
Who was that on the phone?

                    JOHN
The Deacon down at the chapel. Wanted
to – you know –

                    GWEN
Have you offered Hal any refreshments?

                    HAL
No thanks, I'm fine.

GWEN
You're sure?

HAL
Oh, yes.

Phone RINGS. Gwen goes.

HAL
When's your train?

JOHN
Two twenty. Lay over in Rochester,
then catch the night train to New York,
change in New York for the Long Island
Line.

HAL
Any idea when you'll ship out?

JOHN
Next year. Late winter, early spring.

HAL
That long?

JOHN
A lot of training, I guess. Getting fit,
marching, drills, and so on.

HAL
Well, be sure and give me a heads up
on what to expect.

JOHN
You bet. I'll be your chief scout.

HAL
Great. By the way, I haven't told Alice
yet. She thinks I just came back to see
you off.

JOHN
My lips are sealed.

Slight pause.

                    HAL
I guess she's pretty keen on this whole
thing...

                    JOHN
I'll say. She's probably told you about
working the switchboard for the railroad.
Learnt the code for the telegraph as well,
and she's down at the Mill right now passing
out fliers on these "Liberty Bonds".

                    HAL
No second thoughts about your going then?

                    JOHN
No. Proud as punch.

                    HAL
I bet.

                    JOHN
Well, I'm family. She has to crow. Me? I'm
just putting one foot in front of the other.
To tell you the truth, I'm kinda anxious
to get going. Waiting, that's the hard part.
I need to put this show on the road. Get
out of everyone's hair.

Gwen appears.

                    GWEN
Better finish packing.

                    JOHN
Oh, right.

A KNOCK on the door.

                    JOHN
Who was that on the phone?

                    GWEN
Kimberly Fletcher.

                    JOHN
Who?

> GWEN

She said you two had an Algebra class
together. I thought it was a bit of a
stretch – so –

> JOHN

Thanks.

Another KNOCK.

> GWEN

Now, who's that?

She goes.

> JOHN
> (to Hal)

I won't be long.

John goes.

> GWEN (offstage)

Sophie!

> SOPHIE (offstage)

Hello.

> GWEN (offstage)

Are you alone? Where's Alice?

> SOPHIE (offstage)

Papering main street with those "Liberty
Bond" fliers. I couldn't compete.

The door closes.

> GWEN (offstage)

What about, Russell?

> SOPHIE (offstage)

He said to tell you –

> GWEN (offstage)

He's not with you?

> SOPHIE (offstage)

No. Some trouble with the machines
at the Mill. But he promised to be here
in time to take John to the Station.

> GWEN (offstage)
>
> I better give him a call. Hal's in the parlor.

> SOPHIE (offstage)
>
> And John?

> GWEN (offstage)
>
> Packing. I'll tell him you're here.
> (calling)
> John!

Sophie arrives in the parlour.

> HAL
>
> Sophie!

> SOPHIE
>
> Hello stranger. Didn't expect to see you here.

> HAL
>
> I heard from Alice that John was heading out. Didn't want to miss the big send off. Got in last night.

> SOPHIE
>
> Well, it's good to see you.
> (noticing grandma)
> Hello.

> GRANDMA LETTY
>
> Hello.

> SOPHIE
>
> What are you knitting?

> GRANDMA LETTY
>
> Socks. For John.

> HAL
>
> She's knitting me a pair as well.

> SOPHIE
>
> Is she?

> GRANDMA LETTY
>
> Oh, yes.

SOPHIE
Any luck on the job front?

HAL
No. How about you? How've you been
keeping?

SOPHIE
Oh, you know. Busy volunteering.

The front door closes offstage.

SOPHIE (cont'd)
Helping John's mother to get out the
vote. The referendum's only weeks away.

Alice enters with a pile of fliers.

ALICE
Oh, Hal, you came! I didn't really
expect you would.

SOPHIE
He got in last night.

ALICE
Last night?

HAL
Too late to call. I hear you've been
papering the town with fliers.

ALICE
I have. Sophie and I spent all morning
outside the Mill, waylaying workers.

HAL
Any takers?

ALICE
A few. They can't afford the $50 Bond,
but some go for the 25 cent stamps.
16 on a card. When it's full they can cash
it in for five dollars. Fill another ten cards
and they've enough for the fifty. They all
seem keen to do their bit.

                    HAL
And the switchboard job at the railroad
office, How's that going?

                    ALICE
Alright. I just took it for the experience. My
real goal is to be selected by the army for
work overseas. Early days but I've put in my
application and guess what, I'm being
investigated by the Secret Service.

                    SOPHIE
No kidding? Are you really?

                    HAL
Why?

                    ALICE
To verify my loyalty. Then there's a
Psych Test I have to take to prove I
can work under pressure. So – no
guarantees. At the moment they're
recruiting bilingual girls, French and
English. But maybe down the road things
might open up for the rest of us. Anyway,
it's great to see you Hal. I'm so glad you
came. You are sweet.

John enters.

                    JOHN
Well, the gang's all here.

Everyone greets him at once.

                    JOHN
Hi Sophie.

                    SOPHIE
Ready to go?

                    JOHN
As ready as I'm going to be.
            (to Alice)
Where's dad?

ALICE

Still at the Mill, but I'm sure he'll be here
any minute. Sophie and I couldn't wait
any longer so caught the street car.

SOPHIE

Then Alice decided to paper main street
with fliers on the walk home. I was
afraid I might miss you, so went on ahead.

Gwen enters.

GWEN

Alice, could you help me make a few
sandwiches for John to take on the train.

ALICE

Oh, sure. Hal, come along and keep me
company.
          (to Gwen)
Did you get a hold of dad, mother?

GWEN

He said he was just leaving.

ALICE

I hope so.

GWEN

Come along then.

Gwen, Alice and Hal go, leaving John and Sophie alone
with the ever watchful Grandma Letty.

SOPHIE

It's hard to believe you're actually
leaving.

JOHN

I know. I can't believe it myself.

Slight pause.

SOPHIE

I haven't mentioned it before, but I
may be leaving too.

JOHN

When?

SOPHIE

Not sure.

JOHN

Where?

SOPHIE

Well, you remember Ida Saunders?

JOHN

I think so. Vaguely.

SOPHIE

Well, she's taken a job at a factory in
Pennsylvania – doing war work, you know.

JOHN

Oh, yes.

SOPHIE

Yes. And she asked if I would be interested.
She's living with two other girls and they
need a fourth to make the rent.

JOHN

Well, that is news. What kind of work
will you be doing?

SOPHIE

Ida works as a loader, so I guess that's
what I'll be doing too. After I've been
trained up, of course.

JOHN

Loading what?

SOPHIE

Artillery shells. She told me all about
it, about the amatol and TNT.

JOHN

It's – a munitions factory?

SOPHIE

Right. I think it's really important work.
And, like you, I want to do something
important, something that will really
make a difference, make a contribution
to the war effort.

JOHN

Have you told your parents?

SOPHIE

Oh – some. They're okay with it. They've
got their hands full with the younger
kids. I expect they'll hardly miss me.

JOHN

I wish you'd told me before.

SOPHIE

You'd have only tried to talk me out of it.

JOHN

You're right there.

SOPHIE

Oh, John, I was hoping – you'd admire me,
the way I admire you – for stepping up.

JOHN

I do admire you. I don't need you to
do this to get my admiration. You have
it. In spades.

SOPHIE

I know, but – I need to do it for myself.
For the country. Suddenly, women are
needed just as much as men. Wanted even.
It's a great opportunity.

Pause.

JOHN

But it's dangerous.

SOPHIE

Not half as dangerous as it will be for you.

Front Door SLAMS offstage.

RUSSELL (offstage)
I'm back! Let's get going!

Russell enters.

RUSSELL
Where's your mother?

JOHN
In the kitchen with Alice and Hal Newbury.

RUSSELL
(calling)
Gwen!
(to John)
Sorry I'm late.

He sits.

RUSSELL (cont'd)
It's these new two needle machines
that just arrived at the Mill.
(noticing Sophie)
Hello there, Sophie.
(to John)
Ordinarily, we use single needle machines.
But the army requires a double stitch
for all their uniforms.

GWEN (offstage)
(calling)
Is that you, Russell?

RUSSELL
(calling)
Who else?

SOPHIE
You're making uniforms for the army?

RUSSELL
Hope so. We've ordered these machines
on spec, hoping to get a government
contract, which is no easy thing I can tell
you. If not, we'll be stuck with the machines.

Gwen enters, followed by Alice and Hal.

GWEN
Are you still going on about that contract?
I wish your brother had never talked you
into bidding for it

RUSSELL
So do I.
            (noticing Hal)
Hello there, Hal! Surprised to see you here.
I thought you were –

HAL
Well, I wanted to support the troops.

RUSSELL
Of course. I imagine you'll be trooping
off yourself before long.

HAL
Could be.

ALICE
Really?

RUSSELL
John, better put your gear in the
roadster.

JOHN
Right.

He goes.

RUSSELL
Who's all going to the Station?

GWEN
Not me.

RUSSELL
Really. Why not?

GWEN
I'd rather say goodbye here.

RUSSELL
In that case we might all fit. Alice,
why don't you and Sophie and Hal
jump into the roadster. John and I will
be with you in a minute.

Alice, Sophie and Hal all troop off.

RUSSSELL
Are you sure you won't come?

GWEN
I'm afraid I might make a scene and
embarrass myself.

John appears with his gear.

RUSSELL
Here, son, let me give you a hand
there.

He takes the gear and goes.

JOHN
Aren't you coming to the Station, mother?

GWEN
No, I'll stay here with Grandma Letty.

JOHN
Oh, well –

GWEN
Be sure to write.

JOHN
I will ... Goodbye then.

They hug.

GWEN
Goodbye son.

JOHN
The whole thing will probably be over
before I get there.

GWEN
Let's hope.

JOHN
Well, I'd better –

GWEN
Yes.

John goes. Gwen stifles a sob, then anxiously rushes off.

Quickly, Grandma Letty rises and opens the lid of the Victrola.
On a shelf beneath the Victrola she pulls out a vinyl record
and places it on the turntable. "Over There" begins to play.

Gwen rushes out holding a brown paper bag aloft.

GWEN
(calling)
You forgot the sandwiches!!

John races on, grabs the bag and races off.

Grandma Letty joins Gwen. Together they wave to the roaring roadster pulling
away.

"Over There" swells. Lights fade to black.

END OF ACT ONE

ACT 2

Scene 1

Months later.

The Gordon home no longer has its
former solidity.

A weather beaten U.S. flag hangs from
the yardarm.

A portion of the porch is there and
the wicker love seat. Little else.

Upstage a winged backed chair or two can
be seen as well as the Victrola cabinet.

But the stage area itself is more of a
"No Man's Land", a universal space.

The sound of the roadster approaching
brings Gwen on to the porch. She carries
a mixing bowl and spoon, stirring occasionally.

                    GWEN
        Is that you Russell?

We hear the car door slam.

                    RUSSELL (offstage)
        Who else?

                    GWEN
        Oh, Russell – did you hear the news?

Russell appears carrying an armful of firewood.

                    RUSSELL
        What news?

                    GWEN
        The news about –

                    RUSSELL
        If it's bad, I don't want to hear it. I've
        had a terrible day.

He climbs the porch steps.

                    RUSSELL (cont'd)
          Not about John, I hope. He didn't drop a
          live grenade on himself, or shoot some-
          one with his Springfield.

                    GWEN
          No, nothing to do with John. It's the
          proposed 19th amendment.

Russell drops the firewood near the side of the porch.

                    RUSSELL
               (breathless)
          Oh, brother –

                    GWEN
          The House passed it by 150 votes.

                    RUSSELL
          This is your news?

                    GWEN
          I thought you'd be thrilled.

                    RUSSELL
          I will be as soon as I catch my breath.

                    GWEN
          Now, if the Senate will only do the
          same –

                    RUSSELL
          That's the fly in the ointment.

                    GWEN
          Why are you so grumpy?

                    RUSSELL
               (wiping his brow)
          My news is not so good.

                    GWEN
          What now?

RUSSELL
Same old, same old. The government is
threatening to cancel our contract if we
don't deliver 25,000 olive drab OD's on
time. We have the cloth and the cotton,
but its taken the new staff awhile to get
used to the machines, old staff as well.
So we're behind.

He pulls the mail out of his back pocket.

RUSSELL (cont'd)
Here. One from John. The other is for
Alice.

GWEN
John! Why didn't you tell me?

RUSSELL
I had my hands full of firewood.

GWEN
(calling)
Alice!

ALICE (offstage)
What?

GWEN
(calling)
Letter!

RUSSELL
There's more wood in the car.

ALICE (offstage)
Who from?

GWEN
(calling)
No idea!

RUSSELL
Where's the wheel barrow?

GWEN
In the shed, I suppose.

Russell starts to leave.

                    GWEN
          Can I read his letter?

                    RUSSELL
          Can't you wait?

                    GWEN
          No.

                    RUSSELL
          Then why ask?

Russell goes. Alice appears.

                    GWEN
          We've had a letter from John and
          here's one for you.

                    Alice
          Thanks.

                    GWEN
          Looks official.

Alice examines the envelope.

                    GWEN (cont'd)
          Who's it from?

                    ALICE
          Let me read it.

Alice reads.

                    GWEN
          I suppose it wouldn't hurt to peek at
          John's letter.

                    ALICE
                 (hushed tone)
          I've – I've been selected!

                    GWEN
          For what?

ALICE
For training with the Army Signal Corps.

GWEN
How exciting. Are you pleased?

ALICE
Pleased? I'm over the moon.

She sits on the step rereading the letter.

GWEN
Shall I read John's letter or wait
for your father?

ALICE
Oh, mother, aren't you thrilled?

GWEN
Probably not as thrilled as you. But
I'm happy that you're happy.

ALICE
(reading)
It says I have to take an oath before
the Justice of the Peace. Or a Notary
Public.

GWEN
Whatever for?

ALICE
Do we know a Justice of the Peace in
Seneca Falls?

GWEN
Your father might. He travels in those
circles.

ALICE
I hope so. I have to bring a notarized
copy with me to the training center.

GWEN
Where's that?

                    ALICE
               (reading)
There's quite a few: New York, Chicago,
San Francisco, Philadelphia. But it looks
like I'm going to Lancaster, Pennsylvania.

                    GWEN
When?

                    ALICE
Three weeks.

It suddenly dawns on Gwen that Alice, like John, will
be leaving home.

                    GWEN
They didn't give you much notice, did they.

                    ALICE
Then I'll be issued with a uniform.
               (reading)
Oh, dear...

                    GWEN
What now?

                    ALICE
I have to pay for it myself.

                    GWEN
That seems harsh. With all the money
the government's spending on the war,
they can't buy you a uniform. How much?

                    ALICE
$250 to $350.

                    GWEN
Gosh, that is harsh. What's a girl to
do who has no money or any means
of getting any.

                    ALICE
The initial pay is $60 a month.

                    GWEN
A pittance. You make as much working
part time for the railroad.

ALICE
It does say that in some hardship cases,
the hometown father's have been
encouraged to cover the cost.

Gwen takes out two photos from John's letter.

GWEN
Oh, look, Alice, John sent two photos.

ALICE
Let's see.

Gwen sits with Alice sharing the photos.

GWEN
Here he is in his uniform.

Upstage lights come up on John in his doughboy uniform.

ALICE
He looks very proper.

GWEN
Doesn't he.

ALICE
What does he say? Read it.

GWEN
(reading)
Dear mother, dad, and Alice, I sent
you a picture of myself in my uniform.
Since you asked.

JOHN
(removing his hat)
Campaign hat. I've also been issued
an overseas cap and a steel helmet.

John displays the cap and helmet.

ALICE
Very nice.

GWEN
(reading)
For your information the cloth is a
mixture of cotton and wool.

                    JOHN (cont'd)
I've also been issued underwear, not
visible, socks, not as good as grandma
Letty's, olive drab OD, shirt and
trousers, puttees or leggings.

John shows off the leggings.

                    GWEN
                 (reading)
Hobnail shoes.

John shows the sole of the shoe.

                    GWEN
                 (reading)
Service coat and blouse. And a trench
coat for winter weather.

John holds up the coat.

                    JOHN (cont'd)
Which I probably won't need right away.

Russell appears with a wheel barrow full of firewood.

                    GWEN
Oh Russell, come and see. John sent
photos.

                    RUSSELL
I can't be looking at photos. I've
got to stack the firewood.

                    GWEN
Never mind. You can do it later.

                    RUSSELL
                 (climbing the steps)
The disadvantage of having a son in
the army is that he's not around to
do the chores.

Russell sits. Gwen hands him the photo.

                    RUSSELL
What's he say?

                    GWEN
          You can read it later.

                   RUSSELL
                  (noticing)
          What's that other one?

                    JOHN
          That's a picture of my gear.

                    GWEN
                  (reading)
          And personal effects.

John displays a rolled blanket, then unrolls it.

                GWEN (cont'd)
          Condiment can compartments folded
          into haversack.

John holds it up.

                    JOHN
          Stored three day rations of salt,
          sugar, coffee, and tobacco for those
          who smoke.

                    GWEN
                  (reading)
          Meat and bacon can, stored meat ration.

                    JOHN
          Other effects. Shaving kit, mess kit,
          soap dish. Then there's the field gear.
          Haversack -
                  (displaying it)
          Pack carrier which is connected to the
          'shelter half' with pegs and tent poles,
          a poncho and blanket at bottom of
          haversack.

                    GWEN
                  (reading)
          Attaching grommets hold the entrenching
          tool and bayonet in the flap.

John displays.

                    JOHN
Shoulder straps attached to the rifle
belt, containing ammunition, 120 rounds,
30 ball ammo in five round clips.

                    GWEN
                 (reading)
First Aid Kit, wire cutters, canteen,
also attached to bottom of haversack or
rifle belt, gas mask, carried in a separate
bag and slung over the shoulder.

John displays all quickly, then slips on the entire gear.

                    GWEN
                 (reading)
Oh, I almost forgot the most important
thing. My M1 Springfield rifle.

John displays it.

                    JOHN
Some of the NCO's are also issued a 45
calibre pistol,

                    GWEN
                 (trying to read)
What's that?

                    RUSSELL
No idea.

                    JOHN
Because the training is so pushed,
some of the guys haven't got their M1's.
But I hear we might train with the Brits
at first and if that happens, we'll be
issued Enfield's. That' s their weapon.

                    GWEN
                 (reading)
Of course, there are the auxiliary weapons
as well: Grenades, stoke mortars, automatic rifles and machine guns. But that's
all to come, I suppose, when we're attached
to a French Division. No idea yet when I
might ship out. Some say early spring. The
Bosche are said to be planning an offensive
around that time. But no one tells us anything. I really don't know.

                    RUSSELL
I think –

                    GWEN
            (to Russell)
Hang on. Almost finished.

                    JOHN
Well, got to go. Scheduled to do some Close
Order Drill and then a twenty mile hike with
full packs, so I guess I better move out as
they say here at Upton. Bye for now. Your
son, John. P.S. I miss you.

John comes to attention, shoulders his rifle and marches off.
In the b.g. we hear 'marching feet". Lights fade on John.

                    RUSSELL
Well, I guess I better stack the firewood.

                    GWEN
Before you do, Alice has some news too.

                    ALICE
Dad, do you know a Justice of the Peace?

                    RUSSELL
What for? Don't tell me you're getting
married. Has Hal proposed? Or worse?

                    ALICE
No, nothing like that.

                    GWEN
She's been accepted for training with
the Army Signal Corps. Show him
your letter, Alice.

                    ALICE
            (handing over the letter)
I have to take an oath and it has to be
notarized.

                    RUSSELL
            (reading)
What's this? $350 for a uniform?

> ALICE
>
> Then, when I arrive at training camp in
> Lancaster, Pennsylvania, they say I'll
> have to take it again.

> RUSSELL
>
> I can read.

> ALICE
> (rising)
> Oh, I'll be late for work at the railroad
> office. A Notary is acceptable too!

> RUSSELL
> (handing over the letter)
> I'll look into it.

Alice clutches the letter and runs off.

> RUSSELL
> (to Gwen)
> They've been taken from us before
> their time.

> GWEN
>
> I know.

> RUSSELL
>
> And both so young.

> GWEN
>
> Yes.

We hear marching feet as lights fade on Russell and Gwen,
and come up on Sophie.

Sophie stands before a hook, draped with work clothes.

> SOPHIE
>
> Hi Alice. Here in Eddystone, P.A. learning
> the ropes, so to speak. We all wear
> boiler suits, which the company provides.

Sophie slips the boiler suit over her street clothes.

> SOPHIE
>
> They also provide wooden clogs for
> our feet.

She slips on clogs.

>   SOPHIE
> Safer, they say. We provide our own
> hair nets, naturally.

She puts on the hair net over her well pinned hair.

>   SOPHIE
> Masks and glasses if we're handling
> chemicals.

She disappears momentarily and returns with a little
cart on rollers. On the cart is a large ARTILLERY SHELL.

>   SOPHIE
> I work in the loading room where Artillery
> Shells are loaded with ammonia nitrate and
> TNT.

Sophie unscrews the cap.

>   SOPHIE
> Next the fuse is inserted and finally
> the detonator, filled with Mercury
> fulminate.

She puts in the fuse.

>   SOPHIE
> Because of the danger the work must be
> very precise. Last January –
>   (pouring in the fulminate)
> before I got here, eighteen pounds of
> of black powder went up, igniting shells
> and destroying buildings. Many killed.

She checks that the screw threads, then replaces the cap.

>   SOPHIE
> Please don't tell John when you write
> to him, if you write to him, he'd only
> worry. I'm afraid he may face much worse
> now he's in France. I haven't heard from
> him. Have you?

Lights fade on Sophie as she wheels the Shell offstage.

The lights then cross fade to Alice, sitting on a high backed stool in front of a switchboard, wearing headphones.

>ALICE
>
>Dear Sophie, you are so brave. I am full of admiration. At the moment I am recovering from my three week training at Lancaster, P.A., sailing to Liverpool, another story, and taking a Channel Packet to Le Harve in the middle of the night...Now I am at AEF HQ Chaumont, outside Paris. (Address below). Very picturesque but little time to stroll around. Already working. Wearing my $350 uniform. Dark blue Norfolk jacket, matching skirt, black top shoes, hat, overcoat, woollen underwear, and get this, black sateen bloomers. This is in case a stiff wind blows our skirts over our heads I guess. The girls are really cheesed off, that's British, means annoyed, I think. I haven't heard from John, but then I don't think he knows I'm here.
>   (answering phone)
>AEF HQ ,.... one moment please while I transfer your call.

(She hits a switch.)

>ALICE
>   (to Sophie)
>Mum's the word about the factory accident by the way. Take care. Alice.

Lights fade on Alice taking another call, and come up on John sitting on an army cot, illuminated by a flashlight.

>JOHN
>
>We had our first contact with the Bosche, (can't say where). The French commander ordered an artillery barrage, 224 pieces pounding away on Bosche positions before we pushed off, then a rolling barrage to cover our advance.

Lights fade up on Russell and Gwen.

>RUSSELL
>   (reading)
>We took 60 casualties, but 300 prisoners.

                    GWEN
Isn't that an awful lot.

                  RUSSELL
Prisoners or casualties?

                    GWEN
Go on.

                    JOHN
We're still training with the French units.
They built a mock up of the village we've
been ordered to take in a few days. I'll
keep you posted.

                  RUSSELL
        (reading)
By the way, have you heard from Hal? Last
I heard he was training at Camp Fremont.
And Sophie, please pass on my new address.
Hope you are both well and dad's got the Mill
sorted.
        (to Gwen)
Not likely.

                    JOHN
Not sure where everyone is or what
they're doing. Please write. Your son, John.

The flashlight snaps off. Lights fade on Russell and Gwen
and cross fade to Hal in doughboy uniform with full pack.

                    HAL
Alice. Heard from your folks that you
were in France already.

We hear the sound of a BOAT WHISTLE.

                    HAL
I'm here at the Hudson River Docks,
about to embark with the rest of my unit.
If I get anywhere near Chaumont, which
I doubt, I'll look you up. But you may
not recognize me. I've lost a whole head
of hair and about fifteen pounds. Please
write and let me know if you are sent
else where. (Address below). Miss you,
Hal.

BOAT WHISTLE TOOTS as lights fade on Hal and come up on Gwen, writing, and Russell, leaning on a push mower.

> GWEN
> Do you want to add anything to my letter?

> RUSSELL
> Don't know. Read it back.

> GWEN
> Dear John, Bad news. The Senate has yet again rejected the 19th amendment. The good news is that President Wilson is now supporting it. I quote, "We've made partners of the women in the war; shall we admit them only to a partnership of suffering and sacrifice and not to a partnership of privilege and right." He also says he sees woman suffrage as vital to the winning of the war.

Slight pause.

> RUSSELL
> Go on.

> GWEN
> Alice has been transferred to Tours.

Lights up on Alice wearing her travelling uniform.

> ALICE
> It is southwest of Paris, the HQ of Service of Supply or Supply of Service.

> RUSSELL
> She's probably already written to him.

> GWEN
> Who knows?
> (reading)
> She's living in a nice stone house with the other girls.

> ALICE
> We work long hours.

> GWEN
> (reading)
> But have a good spirit.

Distant rumbling of artillery is heard over the phone line.

                    ALICE
      We get calls from commanders and
      officers with ever changing details of battle
      plans or operations. And they depend on us
      to pass on these details promptly and
      efficiently or lives could be lost.

                    GWEN
            (reading)
      General Pershing says our work is vital to
      the war effort.

                    ALICE
            (taking call)
      Hello, AEF HQ, Supply of Service.

Grandma Letty appears with a tray of cool drinks.

                  GRANDMA LETTY
      Lemonade Russell?

                    GWEN
            (reading)
      Grandma Letty is busy with her knitting
      ever since John told her his pals were
      were jealous of his dazzling socks.

Lights up on John cleaning his rifle.

                    JOHN
      I didn't mean it.

                    RUSSELL
            (to grandma Letty)
      Don't mind if I do.

Russell takes a glass.

                  GRANDMA LETTY
      Gwen?

                    GWEN
      Thank you.
            (reading)
      We haven't heard from you in some
      time, but –

RUSSELL
No news is good news.

GWEN
Am sure you'll write when you're free.
(sipping drink)
By the way, Hal stopped by before he
shipped out. Wanted to check on your
whereabouts. Oh, Sophie too. She says
she's been assigned to the black powder
room for a few days, filling bullets, I think.

RUSSELL
Cartridges.

GWEN
(reading)
She's now back in the loading room with
her artillery shells.

Lights up on Sophie with an artillery shell.

GWEN
(reading)
Your father and I might go to the Bond Rally
on Saturday, If we do we'll have to take the
bus because of the gas rationing.

RUSSELL
I'm not going. I have to be on hand at the Mill.
I can't go to any rally or anywhere else.

GWEN
You want me to add that to the letter?

RUSSELL
No. Just say we're thinking of him.

GWEN
I guess that's it then.
(to grandma Letty)
Mother, do you want to add anything?

GRANDMA LETTY
No.

Lights fade slightly on the Gordon's and fade up on John, Sophie, Alice and
Hal, each at their respective tasks.

Each speaks directly front. In the b.g. we hear an artillery barrage.

                    JOHN
Now in front of a German Line that is about
35 kilometres long. Advance slowed. Tough
resistance from the Bosche.

                    SOPHIE
I work in a large Plant, covering several acres.

                    RUSSELL
Besides the OD's, we are now making over-
coats. $16 each.

                    ALICE
Six more girls arrived today. So we are now
an even dozen.

                    HAL
Here at Tours with my new outfit. Asked
after Alice, but they wouldn't tell me a
thing. So haven't a clue where she's
gone. Can you help?

                    JOHN
Impossible to bring up supplies, guns,
and ammo because the roads are jammed
with refugees, carts and horses.

                    GWEN
Once again the Senate has rejected the
proposed 19th amendment.

                    JOHN
Part of small groups sent out last night to
assault Bosche machine gun positions.

                    ALICE
Our office here at... (can't say) was bombed
by a German plane. Not too much damage,
but shaken.

                    SOPHIE
Other jobs here include: making detonators,
filling bullets, weighing powder, making
shell casings and painting and stencilling
shells before shipment.

GWEN
It seems I am always on the phone with
one thing or another. Promoting the Liberty
Bonds or newspaper drives or Red Cross
work, and, of course, the suffrage cause.
Are you well?

RUSSELL
Big bonfire night. Almost torched the place.

JOHN
Back in the Line after a three day break.
Heaviest fighting we've seen. High
explosives and machine gun fire from
the Bosche. We answered with our 75's.

The shelling becomes LOUDER AND CLOSER.

SIPHIE
I like to think that every Shell I fill may
save someone's life. Keeps me going.

ALICE
Cold autumn rain.

RUSSELL
Early snow. Lakes are freezing over.

ALICE
Fire in the barracks threatened our Lines.

JOHN
Tough terrain, deep ravines, dense under-
growth, huge shell craters. Bosche well
dug in and camouflaged.

ALICE
A lot of the girls have turned yellow from
the TNT.

RUSSELL
We have a stock of 40,000 yards of olive drab
on hand.

ALICE
We had to evacuate for an hour because of
the fire. Lost two thirds of our Lines.

                    GWEN
Sadly, Grandma Letty has run out of yarn,
another shortage to add to the list.

                    JOHN
Trapped in the ravine for four days.
rescue parties sent but couldn't break
through. Many losses. I haven't heard
from Sophie. Is she alright?

                    SOPHIE
I have jaundice.

                    ALICE
The place was full of smoke.

                    JOHN
Broke the back of the Hindenburg Line.
Bosche on retreat all along the Western Front.

Huge artillery barrage, then a MASSIVE EXPLOSION.

                    GWEN
Haven't heard from you in some time.

                    RUSSELL
Hope all is well.

                    ALICE
No idea what day it is.

VOICES over the barrage overlap.

                    GWEN
Where are you?

                    SOPHIE
Where are you?

                    HAL
Where are you?

                    ALICE
Where are you?

                    FULL CHORUS
WHERE ARE YOU?

Barrage ends. Silence followed by the TOLLING of a single church bell.

The funereal BELL is gradually joined by other BELLS
in a symphony of joy. Lights fade to black.

ACT 2

Scene 2

Gordon Home. A few more furnishings,
but walls are absent.

Time: Early June, 1919

Church Bells fade into a phone ringing.

Lights come up on Gwen seated near the phone table.

> GWEN (on phone)
> Yes, it is great news! I can hardly believe
> it myself.,, especially as the Senate already
> rejected it five times. I don't know. Perhaps
> the president's prodding had something to
> do with it...And the war, yes, a great factor
> I think. We shamed those men by our
> unprecedented service....Indeed we did,
> Molly....Of course, it's not over. It needs to
> be ratified, and that could be a hard slog. It
> won't be easy to get 36 states to approve
> women's suffrage, which is why we need you
> and others like you in Albany. If New York
> ratifies early, it could set an example, lead
> the way for other eastern states to do the
> same....Yes, with Alice – hopefully. .. Back,
> yes, in body if not in mind. Restless as a
> kitten. I think she got used to a faster pace
> over there than Seneca Falls can offer. Jumps
> every time the phone rings....Ida McPherson
> for one and Abigail Shipstead for another. But
> we need all the support we can muster to
> pressure the New York legislators to do the
> right thing. This may be the one good thing
> to come out of the war....it's true. The Versailles
> Treaty is harsh and the Senate is holding up
> the League of Nations despite the president's
> efforts .... John? Finally back,, yes. Much the
> same. Doesn't say much, won't talk about the
> war. I got more from his letters. Anyway, Molly,
> if you could bring your powers of persuasion to
> Albany...

Lights fade on Gwen and come up on Hal and Grandma
Letty sitting on the porch

GRANDMA LETTY
Were you with John over there?

HAL
No, I never made it to the Front.

GRANDMA LETTY
He was wounded, you know.

HAL
Yes, Alice told me.

GRANDMA LETTY
She should be here soon....needed to go to
the drugstore, pick up some bits and bobs.

HAL
You said.

GRANDMA LETTY
Going to Albany with her mother.

HAL
Uh-huh.

GRANDMA LETTY
No idea why. You'll have to ask Alice.

HAL
I will.

GRANDMA LETTY
She was in France, you know.

HAL
I know.

GRANDMA LETTY
Oh?

HAL
As a matter of fact we were at the same
Camp, but not at the same time.

GRANDMA LETTY
Oh, what a shame.

                    HAL
It was, yes.

                    GRANDMA LETTY
Where did she go?

                    HAL
Up near Verdun, she said. Not far from
John's unit.

                    GRANDMA LETTY
Really.

                    HAL
Yes, you'll have to ask her about it.

                    GRANDMA LETTY
Oh, I don't like to bother her. She did tell
me she was very busy over there, answering
calls, and calling others with messages.

                    HAL
Uh-huh... How's John?

                    GRANDMA LETTY
Seems alright. Limped around for awhile,
but lately he walks without the cane.

                    HAL
Good to hear.

Slight pause.

                    GRANDMA LETTY
Would you care for a refreshment?

                    HAL
No, that's alright. Don't trouble.

                    GRANDMA LETTY
No trouble.
        (rising)
How about coffee? I'll make a fresh pot.

                    HAL
Oh, well –

                    GRANDMA LETTY
And a biscuit. I'll see what we've got.

As Grandma Letty starts to leave, John appears.

> JOHN
> Hal! What are you doing here?

> GRANDMA LETTY
> He came to see Alice.

Grandma Letty goes.

> JOHN
> The illusive Alice.

> HAL
> I'll say. I can't keep up.

> JOHN
> That's Alice.

> HAL
> Where you been?

> JOHN
> Walking.

> HAL
> Oh, sure. Glad to see you're up and
> doing.

> JOHN
> Yes, now I have no excuses.

> HAL
> Pretty rough in the Argonne, I guess.

> JOHN
> Oh well – you know.

> HAL
> No, I don't.

> JOHN
> You didn't miss much.

> HAL
> I read where your outfit was trapped in
> a ravine for a few days.

                    JOHN
That's it. We got about a mile ahead of
the rest of our Division – got out flanked.
Took four days before anyone could break
through and pull us out.

                    HAL
72 percent, I read.

                    JOHN
Sounds right.

                    HAL
I can only imagine.

                    JOHN
Well – over now.

                    HAL
That's it. Pick yourself up, dust yourself
off – any plans?

                    JOHN
You sound like my father.

                    HAL
Sorry.

                    JOHN
How about you?

                    HAL
A dozen, but hard to settle on one thing.

                    JOHN
Yeah, that's it.

                    HAL
Of course, my dad wants me to go into
the family business, but –

                    JOHN
What?

                    HAL
Too much like being in the army, I'm
afraid. Always under the thumb of the
old taskmaster..... He still thinks I was
foolish for not beating the draft.

JOHN

It doesn't really matter what he thinks,
does it?

HAL

No, you're right.

JOHN

You were there. You served. Don't let him
take that away from you – or anyone else.

HAL

You're right.

JOHN

The world's your oyster.

HAL

If you say so.

JOHN

No, if you say so...how's it going with
Alice?

HAL

Not sure. Hard to compete with France.

JOHN

France?

HAL

You know. – France and all the rest. If the war
hadn't come along, I think we were a shoo in.
There were no other options on the table, for
either of us. But – that time has come and gone...
What about you and Sophie?

JOHN

Hell, I don't know. I don't know if she does
either; you know what she told me. She
told me every time she filled an artillery shell
with explosive 'D', she thought of me, that
she might be saving my life. But now that I'm
here in the flesh, I'm not sure she feels the same
way. I mean she had her own war, saw death
up close. Now all she wants to do is party.
I can't do that. She's on a rocket to the moon.

Sophie, with a new hairstyle, is suddenly there.

>   SOPHIE
> What are you two Vets going on about?

>   JOHN
> Sophie! Where did you come from?

>   SOPHIE
> The kitchen. Your mother's been trying to
> recruit me for her trip to Albany. She has
> some fantastic idea that because I worked
> around rockets, that I can put a rocket
> under a few of our legislators and send the
> 19th amendment into orbit.

>   JOHN
> Are you going?

>   SOPHIE
> Not sure. Do you have a better offer?

She takes a cigarette from her bag and lights up.

>   HAL
> I'll just check on the coffee.

Hal goes.

>   JOHN
> You smoke?

>   SOPHIE
> Why not?

>   JOHN
> I don't know. It doesn't suit you.

>   SOPHIE
> Listen, Captain, I've been inhaling toxic
> fumes that make this cigarette look
> like a cure all. You should have seen me
> when I turned yellow from the TNT.
> not that I was alone. Everyone had it. It
> was all the rage.

She takes a drag.

SOPHIE
So what's it to be? Albany? Or the Lakeside
dance tonight? There's a jazz band and some
of my roommates from the loading room are
coming. We're going to dance till dawn.

JOHN
Sounds tempting, but –

SOPHIE
No excuses.

JOHN
Honest, Sophie, I'm not up to it.

SOPHIE
You could come and watch.

JOHN
You're kidding.

SOPHIE
Of course I'm kidding. I know it was
tough for you over there. I know you
hurt. I know you'd rather gaze at the
moon. I know you'd rather put me back
in the bottle, when I was ever so shy.
Sometimes I'd like to go there myself.
But there's no going back. Even if I could,
I don't think you'd notice, or like me
the way you once did. Or was that just
my imagination.

John stares.

SOPHIE
Look, are we still an item or am I wasting
my time?

JOHN
Cut the clowning.

SOPHIE
I would, but I don't think it would help.

JOHN
Help what? What is it that you want?

SOPHIE

I want you to wake up. I want you
to see me the way you used to see
me. I want to go places and do things. I
want you to make a commitment!

JOHN

Uh –

SOPHIE

Not to me. To LIFE. You didn't die in
France, did you? You were lucky, you
survived. If you can't do it for yourself,
then do it for the ones that didn't make
it, or worse – were crippled or maimed –
and can't dance.

JOHN

Dancing till dawn isn't my idea of –

SOPHIE

I'm not talking about dancing. It's a
metaphor!

JOHN

You've been reading again. I told you it
was addictive.

SOPHIE

Better. He's making jokes.

JOHN

Right. I'm a regular Al Jolson.
    (singing badly)
"Rock-a-bye my baby, to a Dixie melody..."

SOPHIE

Spare me the impressions. You have
no future there.

JOHN

Where do you see my future?

SOPHIE

With me. The new me. With all the
trimmings – all the confusion and hope
and love – I can give...What'd ya say?

Pause.

> JOHN
> First – put the cigarette out.

> SOPHIE
> Why should I?

> JOHN
> So I can kiss you.

> SOPHIE
> Fair enough.

She stubs out the cigarette. They kiss lightly and then more passionately.

Suddenly, Alice is there.

> ALICE
> Oh, Sophie, there you are. Mother says you're going to Albany with us.

> SOPHIE
> I didn't say I was going.

> ALICE
> But you must. It's history in the making.

> SOPHIE
> Is it?
> ALICE
> Absolutely.

> SOPHIE
> Oh, in that case, count me in. I've always wanted to be a history maker.

> ALICE
> You'll need an overnight bag. Making history may take a day or two...or three.

> SOPHIE
> No problem. I'll bike home and be back in a jif. When's the train?

> ALICE
> Two-ish. Or thereabouts. Not sure.

JOHN
I'll walk you out.

SOPHIE
Thanks.

Hal appears as Sophie and John start to leave.

HAL
Where ya going?

SOPHIE
Albany.

John and Sophie exit.

ALICE
Hal! Hello. Mother said you were here.
Where've you been?

HAL
Tripping through the tulips with Grandma.

ALICE
How nice. For the tulips I mean. They
love to be appreciated.

HAL
I hear you're off to Albany.

ALICE
That's the plan. Dad's supposed to be
taking us to the Station.

HAL
Oh, I'm sure he'll -

ALICE
You're welcome to come along.

HAL
To the Station.

ALICE
Or Albany.

HAL
Thanks, but –

ALICE
Busy?

                    HAL
That's it...I wanted to see you before
you – wish you – you know...

                    ALICE
I'm glad you did. Sit down, please.

                    HAL
I don't want to hold you up.

                    ALICE
You're not. I'm all packed. Ready to go.

                    HAL
Good.

They sit.

                    HAL
We – uh – haven't really had a chance to –

                    ALICE
Catch up?

                    HAL
That's it.

                    ALICE
I know, I know. I've been all over the place,
like everyone else I suppose. Trying to
figure out what's next, what to do with my
life – now that it seems I'll have one.
Imagine you've been doing the same.

                    HAL
I have, yes. In fact John and I were just
mulling things over.

                    ALICE
Oh, good. He's been very quiet since –
he came back.

                    HAL
Well, I guess he had a pretty tough war
over there.... unlike me,,,

                    ALICE
Oh, you did your bit like the rest of us.
If the war had lasted any longer, you
might not be sitting here.

HAL

I suppose so.

ALICE

No supposing about it.

HAL

Did you know John's outfit was never
really out of the Line.

ALICE

No. He never talks about it.

HAL

So, what about you? How are you –

ALICE

Oh, alright. Still hyper. Every time I hear
a phone ring I race to answer it. Hello,
AEF HQ. Otherwise – I'm good. Getting
on, getting on, I guess. Looking ahead.

HAL

Me too. And when things settle down,
maybe we could pick up where we left
off, before this calamity hit and turned
everything upside down.

ALICE

Oh, Hal, I really can't say. I'm still
trying to get my bearings – to find
Alice. I think I left her somewhere in
France – and I – became something else –
something different.

HAL

Uh-huh.

ALICE

It wasn't a choice. I had to – they needed
me to be different, to leave Alice behind
and think only of the unit, the mission.
They demanded it and we, all of us girls,
thought of nothing else, especially at the
Front. Four hours on, four hours off,
twenty four seven, dead tired. My only
real worry was messing up, not passing
on the right coordinates to a commander,
or losing our phone lines, fighting the
static, yelling to be heard over the roar of
the guns – get it right, get it right, that was
all that mattered.

She smiles.

> ALICE
> So you see, I'm just not ready to... not that
> I'm closing any doors, just trying to say how
> I feel...to be honest with you.

> HAL
> I see that. I see what you're saying. And I
> like what you said about not closing any
> doors – maybe when you get back –

Russell interrupts.

> RUSSELL
> Alice! There you are. Better get your things.
> Tempus fugit.

> ALICE
> Oh, okay.

> RUSSELL
> Hal! Hello. Are you going to this three
> ring circus too?

> HAL
> No.

> ALICE
> Sophie's going.

> RUSSELL
> Sophie! Is she here?

> ALICE
> Any minute. Gone to pack a bag.

> RUSSELL
> How about John?

> ALICE
> Not coming.

Alice starts to go.

> HAL
> (rising)
> Well, goodbye, Alice.

ALICE
Bye, Hal. Thanks for – stopping by.

Alice goes.

RUSSELL
Come again, Hal. Don't be a stranger.

HAL
I will. Thanks.

Hal goes.

RUSSELL
(calling)
Gwen!

Gwen appears.

GWEN
Almost there. You know Sophie's coming.

RUSSELL
I heard.
(checking watch)
Quite a day.

GWEN
Yes, isn't it.

Sophie appears with John.

SOPHIE
Am I late?

GWEN
Not at all.

RUSSELL
John, put Sophie's bag in the roadster,
would you?

JOHN
Sure.

SOPHIE
I can manage.

                    RUSSELL
        No, let him do it. Helps remind the
        lad he's back in civilization.

John takes her bag.

                    GWEN
            Where's Alice?

                    ALICE (offstage)
        Here.

Alice appears with her bag.

                    RUSSELL
            John.

                    JOHN
        I'll get that, Alice.

He takes her bag as well and goes.

                    RUSSELL
        Well, all set?

                    GWEN
        All set.

                    RUSSELL
        To Albany then!

                    GWEN/ALICE/SOPHIE
        To Albany!

Sousa's March, "Stars and Stripes Forever" can
be heard coming from the house.

Granma Letty appears.

                    GRANDMA LETTY
        Hope all goes well.

                    GWEN
        Oh, it must.

                    RUSSELL
                (to Grandma Letty)
        Thanks for the send off!

GWEN
Goodbye Mother!

Russell takes Gwen's bag and leads the troops past John.

RUSSELL
Look at that lawn. Guess I'll have to
give it a haircut.

He coughs meaningfully and disappears with the others.

John joins Grandma Letty on the steps. We hear the
roaster fire up and pull away.

A chorus of 'goodbyes from all accompanies the Sousa
March. John and Grandma Letty wave vigorously.

GRANDMA LETTY
Nice girl. Reminds me of myself when I
was her age.

JOHN
How so?

GRANDMA LETTY
A bright spark. Full of beans.

JOHN
That she is.

GRANDMA LETTY
Wisdom will come later, I suppose.
(to John)
You better get after that grass, John.

JOHN
Guess I better.

John goes. A wistful Letty is left alone. Lights fade with the rousing music.

THE END

A MORE PERFECT UNION

A Play

By

Michael J Shannon

Author's Note

The notion for this play came from a 40's film, "The Talk of the Town". What intrigued me about this comic/drama was the theme of justice redeemed; in this case redeemed by a potential Supreme Court Nominee.

So I focused the play on the judge, Preston Wallace, rather than the escaped prisoner, Yeager, and his childhood sweetheart, Dale Hardy, and started the action in Washington.

A week or so later, this same advisor shows up at the judge's summer rental, (Dale's cottage as it happens)only to discover that her judge has been hijacked by the escaped prisoner, Yeager, and impelled to take on his appeal at the point of a gun. Wallace has dutifully down-loaded Yeager's Texas trial transcript and has found discrepancies that could be used to get a new trial. Marcy, desperate to get the judge back to Washington, calls the president and fills him in.

Meanwhile Yeager and Dale grill Wallace on his upcoming appearance before the Senate Judiciary Committee. Laws and precedents fill the air. Marcy reports that the president is calling the 5th Circuit Court, the court that would handle Yeager's appeal.

Weeks later: Yeager and Dale wait in a motel room, watching Wallace on ESPN, deliver his opening statement before the Senate Committee. During the statement, the Feds arrive and pick up Yeager.

The preamble to the Constitution reads, "In order to form a more perfect Union..." Clearly the Founders realized that the Union was not perfect, but a work in progress.

CAST OF CHARACTERS

MARCY GRIER   U.S. presidential legal advisor. 40's.

PRESTON WALLACE   District Judge, potential Supreme Court
                        nominee. Late 50's.

DALE HARDY   Independent, bright, former childhood
                        sweetheart of Tom Yeager. Late 20's.

TOM YEAGER   On the run from the law, late 20's, early 30's.
                        Seeking refuge and justice..

A MORE PERFECT UNION

ACT 1

Scene 1

Justice Department, Washington.

Office of MARCY GRIER, assistant
legal counsel to the President.

There are two chairs D.R. with a small
table between them.

MARCY, forty something, smartly dressed,
glasses, hair up, polished, flips through
her IPAD making notations.

FEMALE VOICE (intercom)

Preston Wallace.

PRESTON WALLACE, dressed smartly
for the interview, a formality which belies
his more casual preference, enters with
a briefcase.

MARCY
(rising)

Professor Wallace. Delighted. Marcy Grier.

(They shake hands.)

MARCY

How was your flight?

WALLACE

Fine.

MARCY

Hotel?

WALLACE

Fine.

MARCY

And you found our driver this morning
without any trouble?

WALLACE

Fine.

                    MARCY
Good... good of you to take the time
to see us.

                    WALLACE
Well, when Washington calls -

                    MARCY
Have a seat.

                    WALLACE
Thanks.

          (They sit.)

                    MARCY
Coffee?

                    WALLACE
No thanks.

                    MARCY
There's juice or water?

                    WALLACE
No. Thanks...Will the Attorney General be
joining us?

                    MARCY
No.

                    WALLACE
Oh.

                    MARCY
Is that a problem?

                    WALLACE
No. it's just that he briefed me in Chicago....

                    MARCY
I know. I saw his notes on the meeting as
did 'POTUS'.

                    WALLACE
POTUS?

                    MARCY
The president.

                    WALLACE
The president

MARCY

Yes, he's very hands on. Wanted to see all the research.

WALLACE

On what?

WALLACE

Well - on you.

WALLACE

I've been researched by the president?

MARCY

Well yes, of course.
            (after a moment)
Perhaps i should ask you up front before we begin - is there anything we missed? Anything in your background that might be embarrassing either to you or to the president?

WALLACE

Like what?

MARCY

Anything at all. Anything - illegal?

WALLACE

Do you think I'm some kind of security risk? Is that it?

MARCY

Oh no. This is just standard operating procedure for anyone being considered for a high profile job like this...We've uncovered nothing at this point, but if there's anything you're worried about - ?

WALLACE

No, not that I can think of.

MARCY

Fine ... if anything comes to mind, you'll tell us.

WALLACE

There's nothing, really.

MARCY

How about traffic violations?

WALLACE

Seriously?... does that...alright, yes. . I
had three moving violations in one year.

MARCY

Yes, we saw that. Your license was
suspended for two months.

WALLACE

I was just a kid.

MARCY

Twenty two.

WALLACE

Bad luck really...I drove down a one way street
the wrong way...it was night, dark...I was
disoriented...lost.

MARCY

Nothing since then?

WALLACE

No. Clean...You know I went through all
this when I was appointed to the 7th Circuit
Court two years ago.

MARY

I have to ask. Sorry.

WALLACE

The other occasion was a speed trap. You
know, country road...speed limit jumps from 45
to 15, like that.
          (snapping his fingers)
Blink and you miss the sign.

MARCY

And you blinked.

WALLACE

Apparently. The only police car in the County
was waiting at the bottom of a hill as I zipped
by...Had to pay on the spot or go to jail, cash,
no credit cards. Not that I had a credit card
in those days. Cost me ninety five bucks. Be
more like three hundred today. A real racket.

          (He chuckles nervously.)

MARCY

Do you like the police?

WALLACE

Oh yes, generally... it's - uh - very tough
job...made even more so now that automatic
weapons are legally available...Police and
citizens can't become adversaries. I saw this
happen when I was a County Prosecutor...
It's the law that's at fault, not the police,
many of whom I've come to know and
admire.

(Pause.)

MARCY

Let me put you in the picture. And this is
strictly confidential. Well - as confidential
as anything can be in this town.
(after a moment)
At the end of the Court's current session,
Bolton will be resigning.

WALLACE

Judge Bolton?

MARCY

That's right. Not even his colleagues have
a clue.

WALLACE

Mum's the word then.

MARCY

Exacta mundo.

(Slight pause.)

WALLACE

Why tell me?

MARCY

For the past several months, even before
we knew about Bolton's retirement, we
have been putting together a short list of
possible replacements.

WALLACE

Oh...

MARCY

As you know, it's incredibly important to the
future of the country that we choose -

                    WALLACE
Uh - huh.

                    MARCY
You see, the question is: Are we to have a
court that rolls back the gains made in civil
rights, voting rights, privacy law, law enforce-
ment and so forth...since the days of the Warren
Court? Or are we going to reverse these gains
inch by inch by ignoring precedents and adhering
to a narrow interpretation of the Constitution?

                    WALLACE
Uh - huh.

                    MARCY
The point is - this appointment is crucial.

                    WALLACE
Of course.

                    MARCY
We have to be certain.

                    WALLACE
Well, if there's anything I can do to help, I'd -

                    MARCY
During our search your name came up.

                    WALLACE
My name?

                    MARCY
You seem surprised.

                    WALLACE
I am.

                    MARCY
You had no suspicion?...When we spoke on
the phone?

                    WALLACE
No, I assumed...as you said...

                    MARCY
Not even when your driver picked you up
at the 'Seven Eleven' instead of your hotel?

                    WALLACE
Never made the link.

                    MARCY
Really?

                    WALLACE
Went right by me...'Seven Eleven'...Justice
of the Supreme Court. Not a clue.

                    MARCY
Apologies for the subterfuge.

                    WALLACE
Hey...

                    MARCY
Security is imperative.

                    WALLACE
I think I will have that water.

                    MARCY
Help yourself.

          (Wallace takes a bottle of water
          and knocks it back.)

                    MARCY
Are you alright?

                    WALLACE
Fine...So, this is not about a job at Justice?

                    MARCY
No.

                    WALLACE
It's about Bolton's replacement.

                    MARCY
Yes...Is that something you would be prepared to take on - if it were offered?

                    WALLACE
I hadn't thought. This is pretty much out of
the blue.

                    MARCY
You never considered it?... in the back of
your mind?

                    WALLACE
No.

MARCY

Or in your dreams?

WALLACE

Frankly - being a Supreme has been a wish - as long as I can remember...but beyond all - expectation. I -

> (Pause. Wallace is so over-whelmed he can't speak.
>
> After a moment, he hiccups.)

WALLACE

Got the hiccups.

MARCY

Hold your breath.

WALLACE

Does that work?

MARCY

Sometimes.

> (He hiccups again, then holds his breath. Long pause. He exhales.)

MARCY

Better?

WALLACE

I think so.

MARCY

Good.

> (He hiccups.)

MARCY

As you know, if you are... selected, you'd be vetted by the Senate.

WALLACE

Yes, of course.

MARCY

Your life and your record would be scrutinized. Is that something you'd be willing to face?

> (He thinks momentarily, then hiccups.)

MARCY
Perhaps i should say, is that something
you could take on whole heartedly?

WALLACE
Yes...i think so.

MARCY
We'd help you, of course, to avoid the reefs
and the shoals.

WALLACE
Thanks.

MARCY
Do you have any questions?

WALLACE
Not to my knowledge.

MARCY
If you do, you'll know soon enough. How
about guns?

WALLACE
How about them?

MARCY
Do you own a gun?

WALLACE
Do you think I need one?

MARCY
Oh, no - not for protection. At least let's hope
not. It's just that 'gun rights' is a volatile issue.
You might think about getting a hand gun or at
least a rifle. Go hunting.

WALLACE
Hunting?

MARCY
In case you're asked by the Judiciary Committee.
          (after a moment)
You don't have to shoot anything...

WALLACE
Thank you.

MARCY

But you're sure to be asked your views on
gun rights, the 2nd amendment, and the
Heller decision. You're familiar with that
case, I'm sure.

WALLACE

Oh yes. Trumped two hundred years of
prior judicial opinion. Stood the 2nd amendment on its head.

MARCY

I wouldn't say that.

WALLACE

Why?

MARCY

I mean to the Judiciary Committee.

WALLACE

Oh.

MARCY

Just remember that neither I nor the Judiciary
Committee can ask you directly how you would
vote on any given issue or precedent. Anyway
we'll talk about all this if things go ahead.

WALLACE

Alright.

MARCY

One thing they can and will ask you is: What
kind of Justice you'll be? Or: What is your
judicial philosophy?

WALLACE

Well -

MARCY

Are you, for example, an originalist, a strict
constructionist, a constitutionalist, a
majoritarian or a minimalist?

WALLACE

Golly. Not sure.

MARCY

Good answer. The less said the better.

WALLACE

Seriously, I really don't know.

MARCY

Well, for example, some feel that the role of
a judge should be limited, that he or she is not
there to legislate, but to execute the laws. Others
feel that the Framer's intent was to form a more
perfect Union that would become more perfect
in time. The originalist view leans more toward
the idea that the Framer's were more like God.
They saw everything they had made and behold
it was very good. So there's no need to monkey
around with the Constitution.

WALLACE

Well -

MARCY

No need to answer. I'm just throwing it out
there to give you an idea of the judicial
landscape...

WALLACE

I don't think I'm a strict constructionist or an
originalist, but I might be a minimalist or a
fundamentalist.

MARCY

A fundamentalist? Not in a religious context?

WALLACE

No, no.

MARCY

Do you go to church?

WALLACE

Occasionally.

MARCY

Mainstream?

WALLACE

Protestant.

MARCY

That's hardly mainstream.

WALLACE

May I ask a question?

MARCY

Of course.

WALLACE

Why me?

MARCY

Frankly, the president needs someone who
will be approved by the Judiciary Committee
without a cat fight. You have no party affiliation,
your paper trail as an Appellate Judge is minimal,
you were a prosecutor, a professor, went to the
right schools and you're from the mid-west -
which denotes corn, cattle and good sense.

WALLACE

I get it. Not so much my positives as my
minimalist negatives will put me over the
top...so to speak.

MARCY

Exactly... unless, of course, I missed something
besides those traffic tickets. No sex, drugs and
rock'n roll?
                    (slight pause)
Professor?

WALLACE

I have had sex...I'm also a minor drug user -
aspirin being my drug of choice. And I lean
more toward classical music than toward
Taylor Swift.

MARCY

Perfect.

(He shrugs, still bewildered.)

WALLACE

I didn't even know the president knew
I existed.

MARCY

He didn't. But Connors in Justice did.

WALLACE

Terry Connors?

MARCY

Yes.

WALLACE
We worked in Minneapolis together.

MARCY
Putting down bad guys. We know. And
you 'clerked' for Justice Milton.

WALLACE
I did.

MARCY
Milton taught Constitutional Law at Stanford
when the president was a student there...
Your name came up.

WALLACE
(smiling ruefully)
I never worked so hard in my life.

MARCY
He remembered you. Said you were a
lousy golfer.

WALLACE
Justice Milton was a three handicapper. He'd
drag me to the course on my one day off just
to humiliate me.

MARCY
Well, you come highly recommended, judicially
speaking.
(on phone)
Have them bring the car around to the Tenth
Street entrance.
(hanging up)
Shouldn't be long.

WALLACE
What?

MARCY
My car. I think we're about done here.

WALLACE
Oh. RIght.

MARCY
I assume you'll be available, not going
abroad or disappearing down a rabbit hole
any time soon.

                    WALLACE
Well, I've taken a cottage on the Cape for
the summer. Do some writing while the
Court's in recess.

                    MARCY
Nice. Any cases on your fall docket that
might have political ramifications?

                    WALLACE
No, I don't think so. Well, possibly on the
pipe line suit, "Total vs. South Dakota".

                    MARCY
You might want to recuse yourself from
that one. And any others that might
define your judicial philosophy, particularly
any 14th amendment or 4th amendment
cases, which, as you know, can be hot
beds of cultural division.

                    WALLACE
When do you expect a decision?

                    MARCY
No way of knowing. Could be next week, next
month, or god forbid, next year. Much will
depend on the president.

                    WALLACE
I see.

                    MARCY
Once you're settled in your cottage, let us
know your details so we can stay in touch.
If the president has anything specific, I'll
call you on your mobile.

                    WALLACE
Okay.

                    MARCY
If you are nominated, you'll be asked to return
once again. At that time our team will talk
you through the process - role play various
questions that might arise during your testimony
before the Judiciary Committee and steer you,
if necessary, to safer ground - or not, as the
case may be.

        (The phone rings. Marcy picks up.)

MARCY (on phone)

Yes?...Thanks.
        (to Wallace)
That's it then.

(She gathers her gear.)

MARCY

Ever play sports?

WALLACE

Some. High School. College.

MARCY

Really? What did you play?

WALLACE

Ice hockey.

MARCY

The president is an ardent football fan,
particularly college football. I'm sure
you'll get an earful.

(She rises.)

MARCY

All set?

WALLACE

Yes. I think so.
        (rising)
Uh - say, any chance of a lift?

MARCY

You're kidding, right?

WALLACE

No. But if it's a problem, I don't want to
take you out of your way.

MARCY

You won't be. Come on, professor.

WALLACE

Oh, good. Where are you going?

MARCY

To the White House...You too.

WALLACE

Me?

                    MARCY
Yes. He's expecting us.

                    WALLACE
Who?

                    MARCY
The president. He wants to meet you.

              (Wallace stares dumbfounded.)

                    WALLACE
I - I had no idea.

                    MARCY
Don't worry, he's not going to quiz you on
your legal positions or your views on
precedents. He's seen your record. He
just wants to get to know you, size you
up... So relax. Enjoy. This may be your
only chance to meet the leader of the free
world.

              (Wallace hiccups. "Hail to the Chief"
              strikes up.

              BLACKOUT

              The music fades into the sound of
              RAIN, WIND, AND THUNDER.

              CAR WHEELS SCREECH, CRASH.
              POLICE SIRENS BLARE.

              FEET RUNNING, RUNNING,
              RUNNING.)

A MORE PERFECT UNION

ACT 1

Scene 2

BEACH COTTAGE

LIVING ROOM. Wicker furniture,
country rather than stylish.

TOM YEAGER, late 20's, early 30's, with
wet hair, a scruffy beard and clothes that
look slept in, appears from offstage.

He moves to his back pack and takes
out an apple.

Suddenly, he hears the sound of the
front door opening and quickly exits.

                    DALE'S VOICE (ON PHONE)
I'm at the house.

          (Tom re-enters, grabs his back
          pack and exits once again.

          The front door closes loudly.)

                    DALE'S VOICE (ON PHONE)
The cleaners didn't show, the place is a mess
and our renter is moving in tomorrow.

          (DALE HARDY, late 20's early 30's, enters
          with a bag of cleaning materials in one
          hand and a new sponge mop in the other.

          She holds a mobile phone under her chin.)

                    DALE (ON PHONE)
It's only for the summer, mother...Ten grand
makes it worth the aggro, don't you think?...
No, no kids, just the one man...a professor or
judge...we talked about this...

          (She begins to unpack the supplies.)

                    DALE (ON PHONE)
How much damage could he do? He's
a writer. He's writing a book or an article...
I don't know. Something legal, about the law.
He wants total solitude he says.

(She picks up scattered newspapers
and stuffs them in a plastic sack.)

DALE (ON PHONE)
You can't change your mind. If we did that, he
might take us to court, sue us. The man's a
lawyer!

(She throws more debris into
the sack.)

DALE (ON PHONE)
I shouldn't be long. I'm just going to dust,
run the vacuum and the mop around...and -

(Tom appears eating his apple.)

DALE
Ahhhh!

(She drops the phone and clutches
the mop handle like a weapon.)

DALE
Stay back!

TOM
Take it easy.

DALE
What do you want? How did you get in here?

TOM
I remembered you kept a spare key under
the geranium pot.

(Slight pause. She studies him.)

DALE
Who are you?

TOM
Come on, Dale. I know I'm not looking my
best, but -

DALE
How do you know my name?

TOM
You're still the prettiest girl at Central High.
Haven't changed a bit.

DALE

High School. Do I know you from High
School?

TOM

Sittin' in the grandstand,
Beatin' on a tin can,
Who can? We can,
Nobody else can!
Central! Central! Central!

(He bites the apple. Dale lowers
the mop handle.)

DALE

I'm sorry, I don't -

TOM

Senior prom - the beach - waves crashing...

DALE

Ohmygod!...Tom?...Tom Yeager!

TOM

The same.

DALE

You - you look so - different.

TOM

Thank you.

DALE

Oh, Tom...what happened?
          (almost tearful)
Why did you come here?

(She bites her lip, near tears.)

TOM

I was just in the neighborhood and
thought I'd take a chance.

DALE

I can't believe it's you...all these years.

TOM

Yeah, long time...Where's the rest of the
Hardy family?

DALE

Oh, well...dad's gone and -

                    TOM
Oh?

                    DALE
Yes, and mom's with me at my condo. We
rent this place out in the summer. Helps
with the overhead.

                    TOM
Sorry to hear about your dad.

                    DALE
Hmm..
    .   (rattling)
...these beach houses go for a bundle,
even with the chipped furniture. I call it
cozy, comfy living by the sea. I'm in real
estate...sales and rentals...if you're looking
for a place?...I mean - do you plan to stick
around for awhile?

                    TOM
I'm not sure. Sort of playing it by ear...I
was hoping I might hang out with the Hardy's
for a day or two.

                    DALE
Oh - no...that's not possible. As I said the
place is rented. I was just tidying up...
lifting the cobwebs, so to speak.

                    TOM
As it were.

                    DALE
He's moving in tomorrow - the renter.

                    TOM
Oh.

                    DALE
A law professor...writing a book or - something.

        (Slight pause.)

                    DALE
I'd ask you to stay with me, but it's only a
two bedroom and mom has Danny's room.

                    TOM
Danny?

                    DALE
My son ...he's at soccer camp.

                    TOM
Soccer? Is he any good?

                    DALE
He is, he is. I guess he takes after his
father.

                    TOM
Who's the lucky guy?

                    DALE
Gary Schrader. Remember him?

                    TOM
Oh sure.

                    DALE
Not so lucky for me. Things didn't work out.

                    TOM
Oh.

                    DALE
How about you?...Did you ever - settle
down?

                    TOM
No. I've kept pretty much on the move.

                    DALE
Oh.

                    TOM
I joined the Marines - but you knew that.

          (Dale says nothing.)

                    TOM
I wrote...

                    DALE
Are you still - ?

                    TOM
No, my war's over. New battles to fight.

          (She studies him.)

DALE

Are you O.K, Tom? I mean - what are you
doing with yourself these days?

TOM

Oh - surviving.

DALE

It's all over the news...

TOM

Is it?

DALE

You can't stay here, Tom. You have to go.

TOM

In the morning.

DALE

Were you followed?

TOM

I'd know if I was followed.

DALE

Why did you come here? Why? Do you
want to hurt me? Do you want to hurt the
family?

TOM

No, no, that's the last thing I want. I always
liked you and your family...you know that...
I practically lived here.

DALE

You were a stray dog. We couldn't
get rid of you.

TOM

Ruff, ruff!

DALE

Always hanging around - mowing the lawn -
or tinkering with dad's car.

TOM

It was a classic - hard to get parts...but I
did what I could...You still have the old
push mower?

DALE

No.

TOM

Too bad. Nothing better than that push mower.
...have to sharpen the blades every third or
fourth cut though or it starts missing. Ruins
the look - and you need a basket for the
clippings.

DALE

We have a service now. Every Thursday.
They unload, whiz around, make a lot of
racket with their blowers and are gone
in fifteen minutes.

TOM

Some towns outlaw them. Those blowers.
Say the noise is an environmental hazard...

(Pause.)

DALE

You should turn yourself in, Tom. They're
looking for you everywhere.

TOM

I can't..

DALE

Of course you can... I'll drive you. I'll -

TOM

I'd never make it inside. I'd be dead in a
week.

DALE

What are you talking about? That's crazy talk.

TOM

Is it?

DALE

Why did you run, Tom? They say you ran.

TOM

I didn't. Look! The police van got blind sided
by a truck. We skidded, crashed, the van flipped
over. It was unbelievable, like a dream. What
else are they saying?

                    DALE
That you assaulted the Guard.

                    TOM
I never touched the guard. It was the impact
from the crash that knocked him out. I just
grabbed his keys, uncuffed myself and
limped away.

                    DALE
Are you hurt?

                    TOM
No. Did they ever find the truck driver?

                    DALE
I don't know. I haven't heard.

                    TOM
That truck was stolen, you know. Did you
know that?

                    DALE
No.

                    TOM
A stolen truck and the driver disappears. No
trace.

                    DALE
But -

                    TOM
Don't you see - it fits.

                    DALE
What fits?

                    TOM
It was deliberate. A hit and run.

                    DALE
That makes no sense. Why would anyone - ?

                    TOM
I don't know. Maybe - maybe it was a way
to avoid the Appeal. A way to get the case
buried once and for all.

                    DALE
I find that hard to believe.

TOM

I know. You're right. The whole thing is
unbelievable. Absolutely incredible! Not just
the accident. The entire case. All of it. From
the get go. The bomb - the fire - everything!

(Slight pause.)

DALE

You know what you sound like? You sound -
paranoid - crazy.

TOM

Don't...Don''t say that. You remind me of the
prosecutor...dragging up my war years...egg
heads...showing off their lingo...please believe
me, Dale. If you won't, who will?

DALE

How can I believe you? You show up here
out of the blue acting like we were both still
a couple of twelve year olds - reminiscing
about the old days, cars and lawn mowers.

TOM

Because those days were uncomplicated,
innocent days...I'm showing you I haven't
changed. I'm still the same.

DALE

The same boy that broke my heart.

TOM

I plead 9/11 on that front. But on this other...
I swear to God, Dale, I'm innocent.

(A KNOCK on the door. Tom is
immediately alert.)

TOM

Expecting someone?

DALE
(looking out the window)
Must be the cleaners. They said they were
running late.

(She starts for the door.)

TOM

I'll go.

DALE
(stopping)
What?

TOM
Can't be too careful.

DALE
Don't be silly.

(Dale disappears offstage. We hear
the front door open.)

WALLACE'S VOICE
Oh, hi. I stopped by the letting office and
they gave me a key...Preston Wallace...
the - uh - summer tenant.

(Tom slips offstage.)

DALE'S VOICE
Oh, but - I didn't expect you until tomorrow.
The place isn't ready. In fact, it's a mess.

WALLACE'S VOICE
That's alright. I'm not fussy.

(Wallace enters followed by Dale.)

DALE
But -

WALLACE
As long as the bed's comfortable, I'll be
fine.

DALE
But -

WALLACE
I've been on the road the last couple of days
and am absolutely wasted.

DALE
But professor -

WALLACE
And famished. I don't suppose there's anything
to eat?

DALE
Well, no, not much. I was going to stock up -

WALLACE

Never mind. I passed a Convenience Store a
half a mile back -

(He looks out the window.)

WALLACE

Lovely view.

DALE

Yes.

WALLACE

Well, I'll just get my things.

(The front door slams offstage.

Tom enters with two suitcases.)

TOM

Any particular bedroom for the professor,
Dale?

DALE

Oh - uh - the front room, I guess.

TOM

The front room it is.

(Tom exits.)

WALLACE

Well, that's very kind. Is he - ?

DALE

Just an old friend of the family.

WALLACE

Oh.

DALE

Does a little DIY around the place -
occasionally - gardening and - whatever.

WALLACE

I see. Do his services come with the rent?

DALE

No, no. He was just leaving.

(Tom returns.)

                    DALE
Thanks Tom.

                    TOM
No problem. Glad to help.

                    WALLACE
Preston Wallace.

                    TOM
Tom - Tom Wilson.

            (They shake.)

                    TOM
Dale tells me you're in the law. Writing a
book or something.

                    WALLACE
An article...for "The "NLJ".

                    TOM
What's that?

                    WALLACE
The National Law Journal.

                    TOM
Oh, yeah, sure. What's the topic?

                    WALLACE
Well -

                    DALE
Don't bother the professor tonight, Tom.
He's tired from his trip.

                    WALLACE
That's alright. It's called, "Evidentiary Influences
of Emanuel Kant on Approaches in - "

                    TOM
Out of my league, I'm afraid.

                    WALLACE
Are you interested in the law then - ?

                    TOM
Only lately.

            (Suddenly we see FLASHING POLICE
            LIGHTS reflected in the window.)

(Dale and Tom look at each other.
We hear a KNOCK on the door.)

                    DALE

Excuse me.

                    (Dale heads for the door.)

                    WALLACE
                    (being polite)
Any particular area that interests you?

                    TOM
                    (recovering himself)
Uh - Criminal law...Procedure...Equal
Protection - just a hobby. I've been studying
on the side.

                    WALLACE

Have you?

                    TOM
                    (glancing at police lights)
Yes.

                    WALLACE
That's a hard row if you expect to pass
the Bar.

                    TOM
Yes, it's not like the old days when anyone
could pick up Blackstone and then hang
out their shingle.

                    WALLACE
Yes, those were the days. And far cheaper
than law school.

                    TOM.
I guess. What's your field?

                    WALLACE
Constitutional law. Or it was - I'm on the
bench now - 7th Circuit.

                    TOM
No kidding?

                    (We hear the door close and
                    Dale reappears.)

WALLACE

All's well?

DALE

My mother sent them around...We were on
the phone and got cut off. You know, mother,
Tom, always worried - thinking the worst.

TOM

I always liked your mother.

DALE

Let me show you to your room, professor.

WALLACE

Oh, right. Thank you.
          (to Tom)
Goodnight.

          (Dale and Wallace start offstage.)

DALE

I'll let you find your own way out, Tom.

TOM

Sure.

          (We see the reflected POLICE LIGHTS
          disappear as Dale exits with Wallace.

          (Lights fade on Tom.)

A MORE PERFECT UNION

ACT 1

Scene 3

Beach Cottage - early morning

Lights fade up on Tom sitting
in a armchair reading.

Wallace enters and clocks him.

WALLACE
Still here, Mr. Wilson.

TOM
(looking up)
I hope you don't mind.

WALLACE
No. Not exactly.

TOM
This book of yours kept me gripped.
Couldn't put it down.

WALLACE
Book?

TOM
"The Marshall Court, 1801 - 1835"

WALLACE
Where did you find that?

TOM
In your Jeep Cherokee. Along with a pile
of others...I put them in the Study.

WALLACE
Thanks.

(Tom reads.)

WALLACE
Is Ms Hardy around?

TOM
I haven't seen her... Anything you need?

WALLACE
My mobile phone has no coverage.

TOM
Try turning it off and on. That sometimes works.

WALLACE
I tried that.

TOM
Oh.

(He reads.)

WALLACE
Well, I think I'll grab something to eat...Any suggestions?

TOM
There's not much open this early. You might try, "Jesse's", on Beach Road. Used to do a great breakfast.

WALLACE
Beach Road?

TOM
Out the door. Go left to first intersection. Take a right. Eventually you come to another inter-section. That's Beach. Turn left. 'Jesse's' is a couple miles down.

WALLACE
Right, then left...

(Tom nods.)

WALLACE
Would you like to join me?

TOM
No thanks.

WALLACE
Or perhaps I could drop you somewhere. The Bus Station or - ?

TOM
I think I'll stick with Marbury vs. Madison.

                    WALLACE
Well, if you're not here when I get back, let
me just say it was nice to meet you, and
good luck with your legal studies.

                    TOM
Oh, thanks.

                    WALLACE·
Goodbye, Mr. Wilson.

                    TOM
Take care.

          (Wallace exits. We hear the door
          close.

          After a moment we hear the car
          engine turn over, then die. It
          sputters coughs, then dies again.
          More sputtering then silence.

          The door slams. Wallace returns.)

                    TOM
Problem?

                    WALLACE
Car won't start.

                    TOM
Oh?

                    WALLACE
No.

                    TOM
Dead?

                    WALLACE
No.

                    TOM
Not the battery then.

                    WALLACE
No, I'm sure it's not the battery.

          (Slight pause.)

                    TOM
I can have a look if you want.

WALLACE

You?

TOM

If you want.

WALLACE

Are you familiar with - ?

TOM

No, but I'm familiar with engines. Been
around cars since I was a kid.

WALLACE

I think I'll wait.

TOM

Up to you.

WALLACE

Everything's computerized nowadays.

TOM

Computer runs electrics. Your problem
doesn't sound electrical.

WALLACE

What does it sound like?

TOM

Hard to say unless I take a look.

WALLACE

You're not going to - ?

TOM

I'll just have a look.

WALLACE

That's -

TOM

Give it the once over.

WALLACE

It's a six cylinder.

TOM

Yeah, I noticed when I was unloading your
gear last night.

(He rises.)

                    TOM
There should be some tools in the garage.

                  WALLACE
Tools?

                    TOM
Used to be anyway.

                  WALLACE
You won't -

                    TOM
No. A diagnosis, that's all.

                  WALLACE
Okay.

                    TOM
I won't be a minute. Then I'll get out of
your hair.

          (Tom exits. Wallace takes out his
          mobile and checks his messages.

          As he does the front door opens
          and closes.

          After a moment Dale appears with
          two bags of groceries.)

                   DALE
You're up.

                  WALLACE
Yes.

                   DALE
I was hoping to be the early bird and make
you breakfast.

                  WALLACE
I won't say no to that.

                   DALE
I'm still feeling bad about the cleaners not
showing.

                  WALLACE
i did arrive a day early.

                    DALE
You did.

          (She exits with the groceries.)

              DALE (OFFSTAGE)
You sleep alright?

                  WALLACE
A little restless. But more to do with a
growling stomach than the quality of
the mattress.

              DALE (OFFSTAGE)
You must be famished!

                  WALLACE
I am! I was so desperate that I tried
hunting for a local cafe. But my car
wouldn't start.

              DALE (OFFSTAGE)
Oh no! What's the trouble?

                  WALLACE
No idea! Your friend, Mr. Wilson, is having a
look.

          (We hear a CRASH of dishes from
          the kitchen. Then Dale appears
          holding a box of cereal.)

                    DALE
Tom? Tom's here?

                  WALLACE
Yes. Said he'd been around cars all his life.

                    DALE
Was he here all night?

                  WALLACE
Apparently.

                    DALE
I'm terribly sorry. I had no idea.

                  WALLACE
Found him buried in one of my books.

                    DALE
I thought he left.

                    WALLACE
So did I.

                     DALE
I'll see that he goes.

                    WALLACE
Not a problem. How long has he been
here?

                     DALE
Arrived yesterday.

                    WALLACE
I see.

          (Slight pause.)

                     DALE
We have cornflakes or Rice Chexs for starters.
To be followed by bacon and eggs, toast and
coffee.

                    WALLACE
Can't wait.

          (Dale exits to the kitchen. Tom enters
          holding a rag. He wipes oil from his
          hands.)

                    WALLACE
Any luck?

                     TOM
Yes and no.

                    WALLACE
What's the good news?

                     TOM
I think I found your problem.

                    WALLACE
And the bad?

                     TOM
You might need a new water pump.

                    WALLACE
Expensive?

TOM

A water pump is relatively cheap, but
the labor is a big job. Could run your bill
up to a thousand or more.

WALLACE

You're kidding?

TOM

Is it still under warranty?

WALLACE

No, I only got the minimum

TOM

Whoops.

WALLACE

Guess I'll just have to pay the piper.

TOM

I'd also recommend replacing the timing
and drive belts, the coolant, of course,
and you'll need a new thermostat and
radiator cap.

(Dale enters with a tray of cereal
boxes, milk, sugar, cups, etc.)

DALE
(to Tom)

Hello.

TOM

Morning.

DALE

I thought you left.

(She begins to unload the tray.)

DALE

Here you go, professor. This will get you
started.

WALLACE

Thanks. You don't happen to have a water
pump for a late model Jeep Cherokee around
the house?

DALE

Do you need one?

WALLACE

Apparently.

DALE

Check online. That's your best bet. Coffee
now or later?

WALLACE

Now please.

(Dale exits.)

WALLACE
(to Tom)
Would you mind getting my laptop while
I dive into these cornflakes. It's in my room.

TOM

Sure.

(Tom exits. Dale enters with a
coffee pot.)

DALE

Coffee?

WALLACE

Thanks. Do you have wi-fi?

DALE
(pouring coffee)
Oh yes.

WALLACE

I'll need the code when you get a chance.

DALE

Sure.

(Dale exits. Tom enters with the
laptop.)

TOM

Here ya go.

WALLACE

Thanks. Help yourself to coffee.

                    TOM
Thanks.

                  WALLACE
And cereal if you want.

                    TOM
                  (sitting)
Thanks.

          (He pours himself a coffee.

          Dale enters with a platter of
          bacon and scrambled eggs.)

                   DALE
                  (to Tom)
Make yourself at home.

                    TOM
i was invited.

          (Dale puts the platter down.)

                   DALE
Be careful, professor, or he'll scoff the whole
platter before you can get a mouthful.

                  WALLACE
                  (to Tom)
Help yourself, please.

                   DALE
You've been warned.

          (She exits.)

                  WALLACE
How long do you think it will take to get
a new pump?

                    TOM
A day or two. Any part supplier can ship
it express. Or you could get a tow to the
nearest garage and get the garage to place
the order.

          (Dale enters with a platter of toast,
          jam, butter, etc.

          Tom takes a piece off the platter.)

TOM

Ooh! Toast!

DALE

Can't you wait?

(She puts the platter down.)

TOM

Say Dale, is Charlie Fitz still in business?

DALE

No, Charlie folded when the recession hit.
(to Wallace)
Fitz had a garage a stone's throw from here.
Good mechanic.

TOM

A great mechanic and honest. He would have
given you a good price.

WALLACE

Sorry to hear he folded.

TOM

I used to moonlight for him when he needed
help. The man was a genius.

WALLACE

Oh, yes.

TOM

Hmm.

WALLACE

Then perhaps you could do the job - replace
the pump?

TOM

Me?

DALE

I'm afraid, Mr. Wilson, has to be on his way.

WALLACE

Oh.

TOM

Not really.

DALE

What about the other thing?

TOM

What other thing?

DALE

You know.

TOM

Oh that. That can wait.

DALE

Are you sure? i thought you were wanted - needed - elsewhere.

TOM

I could stick around if it would help.

WALLACE

Okay, tell you what. Give me a fair price on the repair and I'll throw in room and board while you're on the job.

TOM

Sounds good.

WALLACE

It's settled then. Now, if you'll excuse me, I need to make a phone call. There's a land line, I believe?

DALE

In the Study.

WALLACE

Thanks. I can't get coverage on my mobile.

(Wallace exits with his coffee.)

DALE
(hissing)
What are you doing here?

TOM

Fixing his pump.

DALE

No you're not. You're going to make your excuses and hit the road.

TOM

I can't. Not in broad daylight.

DALE
You're putting me in a terrible position. Not
to mention the professor.

WALLACE
The professor will never know a thing unless
you tell him.

DALE
I think he's suspicious.

TOM
If he were suspicious, he wouldn't have
asked me to fix his car. Come on, Dale,
two days, tops. I'll fix his pump and I'm
out of here.

DALE
Promise?

TOM
Promise.

(He holds up his fist. She reluctantly
taps it with hers.

Wallace returns.)

WALLACE
The phone's dead.

DALE
Are you sure?

WALLACE
Yes. No dial tone.

DALE
I can't believe it.

TOM
Did your mother pay the bill?

DALE
It's direct debit.

TOM
Coyotes maybe. Chewed the line.

WALLACE
How often do you use it?

DALE

I don't. I use my mobile.

WALLACE

Perhaps I could use that.

DALE

It's in my car.

TOM

Hang on. I'll get it.

(Tom exits.)

DALE

I'm terribly embarrassed, professor. I had
no idea there was a problem.

WALLACE

So it could have been out of order for
some time.

DALE

I suppose so. Why?

WALLACE

Ms. Hardy...I don't quite know how to tell
you this - but I think your friend, Tom, is
wanted by the police.

DALE

Tom?

WALLACE

It came to me last night. But I wasn't sure.
It seemed so - unbelievable... and, of course,
i didn't want to - accuse him if ....

DALE

Accuse him of what?

WALLACE

There was a case in Texarcana. An explosion
at a chemical company, a fire...multiple deaths...
surely you heard about it?

DALE

Yes. something. There was a trial wasn't there?

WALLACE

Yes, and then a dramatic escape during a
transfer from County Jail to State prison.

DALE

Oh yes, I do recall -

WALLACE

I think that escaped prisoner is your friend.

(Pause.)

DALE

I told him to leave. I thought he had. I
said nothing to you, hoping...

(Tom returns with Dale's phone.)

TOM

Here you are, professor.

WALLACE
(glancing at phone)

No coverage.

DALE

Really?

WALLACE

No.

TOM

You might have better luck on the porch
or down by the beach.

WALLACE

You think so?

TOM

Worth a try.

WALLACE

Alright.

(Wallace glances at Dale and then
exits.)

DALE

It's no use, Tom.

TOM

You never know.

(He sits at Wallace's laptop and
boots up.)

TOM

What's the wi-fi?

DALE

Netgear 06482.

TOM

Thanks. I just want to get a price on the
professor's water pump.

DALE

You're sure it's the pump?

TOM

What?...yeah...pretty sure. if not, he can
send it back. There's a special return
policy with most suppliers.

DALE

More coffee?

TOM

I wont say no.

(Dale exits with the coffee pot.

Wallace enters.)

TOM

I'm on the case professor. Checking out various
suppliers. But I'll need the make and model
number to order...

WALLACE

It's a 2018. SV7

TOM

Any luck?

WALLACE

No.

TOM

Could be atmospherics.

WALLACE

Where's Ms Hardy?

TOM

Making coffee.

WALLACE

Oh.

TOM

There's more eggs.

WALLACE

No thanks. My primary concern at the
moment is to find a phone that works
so I can call the police.

(Tom looks up from his laptop.)

TOM

The police?

(Dale enters with the coffee pot.)

WALLACE

Yes. I'm afraid I'm going to have to report
you.

(Tom looks at Dale.)

DALE

He guessed.

TOM

Really.

DALE

I said nothing.

WALLACE

It's all over the news, Mr. -

TOM

Yeager.

WALLACE

Yeager?

DALE

Tom Yeager.

TOM

Is that true, professor? She said nothing?

WALLACE

No. I mean 'yes', it's true.

DALE
You should have left last night, Tom.
Why didn't you?

TOM
I only just got here. It seemed rude.

DALE
That never stopped you before.

TOM
I trekked country roads, waded streams,
slept under bridges, ate ants and beetles
to get here. Leaving so soon was out of the
question.

DALE
You did me no favors.

TOM
I don't suppose it matters that I'm innocent?

WALLACE
Not according to the law.

TOM
The law?

WALLACE
You had a trial. A lawyer. You were convicted.

TOM
I had a Public Defender who was so over
worked and under paid he kept dozing off
during the trial. All he wanted me to do was
to plead guilty and accept a plea deal.

WALLACE
That may have been good advice.

DALE
I could drive you to the station.

TOM
Is that your best offer?

DALE
You can't stay. You're putting me in a terrible
position. Not to mention the professor.

TOM
What about my position?

WALLACE

She's right. Aiding and abetting an escaped
felon is a serious crime.

TOM

I'll cuff you both and put you in the basement.
No aiding and abetting. You're off the hook.

DALE

You have cuffs?

TOM

I took them off the guard.

WALLACE

Let's be serious. What exactly do you
want?

TOM

I want someone to listen to me. To believe
me.

WALLACE

It would do no good. You've been tried
and sentenced.

TOM

There's the Appeal.

WALLACE

Do you really believe the Appeal has a
hope in hell of overturning your conviction?

TOM

I have to believe that.

WALLACE

On what grounds?

TOM

I was railroaded.

WALLACE

That is not a legal defense.

TOM

If it's not, it should be.

WALLACE

Carping about the law will not help you.

                    TOM
No one's carping. Forget carping. I want -
I need - someone to help me level the
playing field. Someone who knows the law
and is willing to -

                    DALE
Tom.

                    TOM
Take my case.

                    WALLACE
That's impossible. I'm not a criminal lawyer.
Even if I were -

                    TOM
Come on, professor. Stand up and fly right.

                    WALLACE
I'm sorry, I can't help. I came here to write,
not to -

                    TOM
There ya go. Take my case and you'll have
something to write about besides Emmanuel
Kant and what was it?

          (Wallace shrugs.)

                    TOM
It'll boost your sales. The publicity will -

                    WALLACE
This is ridiculous! Yours is not the kind of
publicity I need or want. Your case, as you call
it, is a poisoned chalice. The perception, right
or wrong, is that you have transgressed the law
in such a callous way that any kind of sympathy
for you would be received with contempt.

                    TOM
Which is why that perception has to be changed.

                    WALLACE
Not by me. I tell you both in confidence, with
the understanding that it will go no further than
this room, that I am being considered for a
vacancy on the Supreme Court.

                    DALE
Really.

WALLACE
Yes, although the vacancy is not yet publicly
known. A decision is expected any time within
the next two to three months. So you see it is
impossible for me to help you. Even failing to
report your presence here could be fatal to my
chances.

TOM
Look, professor, i don't want to jeopardize your
future, believe me. What I want is a future of my
own.

WALLACE
As far as I can see, you have no future unless
you turn yourself into the police.

TOM
That's not an option. I wouldn't last a week.

DALE
Tom.

TOM
I don't think either of you understand -
there are powerful forces behind this.

WALLACE
That kind of talk will only hurt your Appeal.
It's crazy talk. They'll have you hospitalized
and put under observation.

TOM
They did.

WALLACE
I'm not surprised.

TOM
My lawyer was delighted. Thought an insanity
defense might get me a lighter sentence or
a couple of years in an asylum. No way I was
going down that road.

WALLACE
Were there grounds for such a defense?

TOM
No. But the shrinks and head hunters decided
that I might be suffering from PTSD, you know,
the veterans disease. Too many tours in South-
east Asia. The whole thing is a scam, a cover up.

(Wallace looks to Dale for help.)

WALLACE

Well, as I said, you're treading on very dangerous ground with that line. Conspiracy theories went out in the 80's.

TOM

It's the truth.

WALLACE

You say.

TOM

Damn straight.

WALLACE

I have nothing to suggest.

TOM

Then why pretend to be interested in justice? Knowing the law is nothing unless it is applied and enforced.

WALLACE

I'll keep that in mind.

TOM

What kind of Supreme Court Justice are you going to be?

WALLACE

If you don't leave, I'll never have a chance to find out - assuming I'm nominated.

TOM

Well, I'm sorry, professor, but I can't lay my head on the block to save your career. I need something more.

(Pause.)

WALLACE

If I were to hear you out, look into the matter, would you go?

(Tom nods.)

WALLACE

Very well...do you trust Ms Hardy?

(Tom looks at Dale.)

TOM

Yeah, sure.

WALLACE

Because you quite obviously don't trust
me or the law.

DALE

I -

WALLACE

Yes?

DALE

- cannot get involved in this.

WALLACE

You are involved. Just as I am. That's a given.
What we need now is a team effort to examine
the facts, without prejudice, so Mr. Yeager will
leave us in peace and be on his way...Do you
have a computer?

DALE

Yes.

WALLACE

Good. We will download the trial transcript.
Examine it and determine whether or not there
is a legal basis for a new trial. If we need clarification,
explanations or if any discrepancies arise, we will
ask the plaintiff. Otherwise -
          (to Tom)
- you will not be needed. - other than to install a new
water pump in my Jeep Cherokee.

DALE

Look, I'm no legal eagle. I -

WALLACE

Certainly not, but I am. You will be my protection.

DALE

Protection? From what?

WALLACE

From any lingering doubts that this process has
not been carried out fairly.
          (to Tom)
That's all we can do. We can't guarantee a new
trial or exoneration for your friend.

DALE
Any suggestions as to what to tell my mother?

WALLACE
Tell her you're staying here, that you're
working for me for a few days - at my request.

TOM
Don't mention me.

(Slight hesitation)

DALE
No...I won't.

WALLACE
You haven't, have you?

DALE
No, no...not directly.

(Tom and Wallace stare at her.)

DALE
Just reminiscing ....your name came up.

TOM
She remembers me?

DALE
Oh, yes.

TOM
Nothing more - nothing about - ?

DALE
No, of course not.

WALLACE
Better pick up a tooth brush.

TOM
And some more groceries.

DALE
Any requests?

TOM
Whatever you like. I'm easy.

DALE
You've never been easy.

(Wallace hands Dale a few large
bills.)

WALLACE

Here you are.

DALE

Oh, no.

WALLACE

Please. I insist. I'd like a good Scotch.
Chevas or Johnny Walker Black.

DALE

Right.

WALLACE

And if you could get the phone company
to fix the land line that would be a plus.
Obviously with the atmospherics...
(a glance at Tom)
I can't depend on my mobile.

DALE

Right.

(She gives Tom a quick look
and exits.)

WALLACE

Won't see her again.

TOM

You think...she'll go to the police?

WALLACE

God I hope so.

(We hear Dale's car start and
pull away.)

TOM

I wouldn't blame her if she did.

WALLACE

No.

TOM

It's a lot to ask.

WALLACE

Yes, it is.

(Slight pause.)

                    TOM
I'll just get your Vin number. Order
the pump.

          (He starts to go, then stops
          and turns.)

                    TOM
Thanks...you know.

                    WALLACE
I can't promise anything, you understand
that.

                    TOM
               (near tears)
Still - it's a chance.

                    WALLACE
Does the Jeep really need a new pump?
Or was that just a ruse to keep me here?

          (Tom smiles slightly then shakes
          his head, 'no'.)

                    WALLACE
What about the phone?

                    TOM
If I thought of it, I might have cut the wire.

                    WALLACE
Then it was fate.

                    TOM
I guess.

          (Wallace glances out to sea.)

                    WALLACE
There's no need to thank me. My motives are
hardly -
               (turning to Tom)
What would you do if I walked out of here right
now? Would you try to stop me?

          (Tom shrugs.)

TOM

Probably not...but I'd be disappointed.

WALLACE

The law is not always right, Mr. Yeager...If
it has worked against you unjustly, as you
claim, perhaps it can work for you. The thing
to understand about the law is that it is not
personal.

TOM

It feels personal.

> (Tom exits. Wallace sits at his
> laptop and begins the search.
>
> Lights fade to black.)

End of Act 1

A MORE PERFECT UNION

ACT 1

Scene 1

Two days later.

Food wrappers liter the tables where
Wallace sits bleary eyed in front
of his laptop. He needs a shave.

Dale enters with a mug.

WALLACE

What's that?

DALE

Tea.

WALLACE

Tea?

DALE

Hmm.

(She sits at her own computer.)

WALLACE

Any coffee?

DALE

No, but there's beans and a kettle.

WALLACE

Oh, it's like that, is it?

DALE

Self catering kicks in on day three.

(SHOUTS and GROANS are heard
offstage.)

WALLACE

What's he doing out there?

DALE

Shouting at your car.

WALLACE

Is that common? Or has my car been
singled out for abuse?

(More SHOUTS from offstage.)

DALE

I'd say a bit of both.

WALLACE

You sure he knows what he's doing?

DALE

No.

WALLACE

That's comforting.

DALE

But he's relentless. He'll wrestle with it
until he's solved the problem - whatever
it is. He never gives up.

WALLACE

Maybe he should do this and I should
shout at the car.

DALE

You're not throwing in the towel?

WALLACE
(rubbing his eyes)
I don't know what else to do... where else
to look. It's a maze of contradictions, a
mystery, incomprehensible...on the face of
it the evidence is more than damning, it's -

DALE

He says it's not true.

WALLACE

That won't get him a new trial.

DALE

What will?

WALLACE

I was hoping you'd call the police.

DALE

Maybe I did.

WALLACE

Where are they?

DALE

I hung up.

(Wallace stretches and begins
to walk around aimlessly.)

DALE

You think he's guilty?

WALLACE

If he's not, someone has gone to extra-
ordinary lengths to make him look guilty.
It's not just the forensic evidence. It's
the demolition job done on his character,
his stability, his state of mind, his military
record, PTSD, ad infinitum - all weighted
against him to such a degree that it leads
me to believe that he might very well be -
innocent.That everything he's told us is
true. But how to prove it - ?

DALE

Yes, that's the thing.

WALLACE

It would take a legal team, resources and
money far beyond anything he could
manage. It would take years and in the
end, the effort would probably fail.

(He sips Dale's tea,)

DALE

What about legal aid? Surely something
could be done?

WALLACE

A drop in the bucket. Any family?

DALE

No. His mother died when he was eleven,
his father remarried, had a couple of kids. I
heard they moved away...we sort of adopted
him or rather he adopted us...always hanging
around, underfoot...No one minded...he made
himself useful...Anyway we're getting ahead
of ourselves. The primary thing is the Appeal.

(Pause.)

DALE

If we could prove complicity -

WALLACE

No one would believe it - unless you could
also prove motive.

DALE

For the sake of argument - let's say -

WALLACE

What?

DALE

Bear with me?

WALLACE

That's what I've been doing.

DALE

Please.

WALLACE

Okay.

DALE

If evidence was manufactured -

WALLACE

You're going with Yeager's theory - ?

DALE

- it probably was outsourced.

WALLACE

Which would make it even harder to prove.

DALE

- to a private company or someone who
specializes in this type of thing.

WALLACE

What type of thing?

DALE

Doctoring photos, ID theft, body doubles,
facial masks, pressuring or bribing witnesses.

WALLACE

You think all those witnesses lied?

DALE

Maybe they didn't know they were lying.
Maybe they were just repeating derogatory
information fed to them by the prosecution.

                    WALLACE
All of them?

                    DALE
Maybe -

                    WALLACE
Some of those people were well heeled,
well educated, not easily influenced -

                    DALE
Well, maybe they were told their testimony
was only incidental to the case, that they
were just one of many on an impressive
list - and that standing tall was a chance
to step up to the plate, to be a good citizen.
In that case a lie for a good cause would
be a plus. They'd be admired and appreciated
by all. And if there were any negative re-
percussions, if the defense went after them,
for example, questioned their veracity, the
State would protect and defend them.

                    WALLACE
You're going into a very grey area. And
even if we could prove or cast doubt on
someone's credibility, I don't see an Appeal's
Court reversing the lower Court and certainly
not granting a new trial. It's all too ephemeral.
You'd need some kind of record, a voice re-
cording of the prosecution actually feeding
this line and encouraging potential witnesses
to perjure themselves. Anything else would be
speculation.

                    DALE
What about the DNA evidence? I thought you
said that taking a DNA swab was inadmissible
without a warrant. Surely that would be
grounds for a new trial.

                    WALLACE
i said a swab was controversial, not
inadmissible.

                    DALE
So there's doubt.

                    WALLACE
A DNA swab taken at the point of questioning
or arrest was deemed constitutional in the case
of Maryland vs. King a few years ago.

WALLACE (cont'd)

But it was a narrow opinion. The minority opinion dissented vigorously. Said a warrant-less swab infringed 4th amendment rights.

DALE

So no new trial?

WALLACE

Not on those grounds.

DALE

So there's nothing - nothing we can do.

WALLACE

i didn't say that.

(Tom enters holding a socket wrench.)

TOM

Hey, how's it going?

DALE

Swell.

WALLACE

Great. Dale's turning into a real legal eagle.

TOM

Really?

DALE

No, not really.

TOM

I always said she had a head on hershoulders.

DALE

Beeswax.

TOM

So what's the scoop?

WALLACE

Just working on our strategy.

TOM

Oh.

                    WALLACE
How's things at your end?

                    DALE
We heard you shouting.

                    TOM
Oh, well -

                    DALE
I had to reassure the professor it wasn't
personal.

                    TOM
No, no. Wrench slipped, that's all.

                    WALLACE
Making progress?

                    TOM
I did a pressure test and unscrewed the
cover on the water pump.

                    DALE
That's about where we are.

                    TOM
Just need to take the old pump out and
put in the new one.

                    WALLACE
Good.

                    TOM
Then, you know, put everything back -
ship shape.

                    WALLACE
Excellent.

                    TOM
Shouldn't take long. Two, three hours.

          (Slight pause.)

                    TOM
Is that coffee?

                    DALE
Tea.

                    TOM
Tea?

                    DALE
Hmm.

                    TOM
Oh.

                    DALE
You're welcome to make coffee. Just
help yourself.

                    TOM
No thanks...so...uh - what's the strategy?

          (After a moment.)

                DALE/WALLACE
Well we -

                    DALE
             (to Wallace)
You go.

                  WALLACE
After you.

                    DALE
You're the professor.

                  WALLACE
Alright...well, as you know, the prosecution
case against you is pretty strong. So strong,
in fact, that I think our best bet is to ignore it
altogether.

                    TOM
Ignore it?

                  WALLACE
Yes.

                    TOM
That's the strategy?

                  WALLACE
Just let me -

                    TOM
Two days and -

WALLACE

Give me -

TOM

I laid it all out.

WALLACE

I know.

TOM

Then -

WALLACE

Let me - explain.

(Pause. Tom waits nervously.)

WALLACE

What with the preponderance of forensic
evidence -

TOM

I told you -

WALLACE

Please.

TOM

Sorry.

WALLACE

With the preponderance of forensics, the
video footage from internal security cameras
showing you near the warehouse -

TOM

Doctored.

WALLACE

- the DNA, the fingerprints, the hair fibers -

TOM

Yah - dah -dah - dah - dah - dah!

WALLACE

- the psychiatric report suggesting a dis-
gruntled ex-employee seeking revenge
as a motive for the bombing -

TOM

It wasn't a bomb.

                    WALLACE
Whatever.

                    TOM
It was an accident.

                    WALLACE
May I finish?

                    TOM
Sorry. Please - go on.

                    WALLACE
The only grounds I think might give you a
crack at a new trial is that the publicity
surrounding - the accident - was so adverse,
so overwhelmingly negative, demonizing you
in some media outlets, that it was imperative
that the trial be moved to a different venue...
You P.D.'s motion for new venue was, as
you know, denied by Judge Winthrop, in spite
of the fact that Texarcana is a company town,
employing hundreds, if not thousands, as well
as peripheral employees working for sub-
sidiaries of Chem Co. and dependent on the
company for their livelihoods. Our argument
would say that such saturation limited the
jury pool and made it almost impossible to find
a jury that was not prejudiced against you.

                    TOM
You think the Appeal's Court would buy that?

                    WALLACE
We would also cite irregularities in the
sentencing. The fact that Winthrop allowed
the prosecution to poll the views of potential
jurors on the death penalty. Any juror who
opposed it, didn't make the final cut, thus
prejudging or prejudicing the case.

                    TOM
i still don't - I mean, what about Chem Co?

          (Slight pause.)

                    DALE
The professor doesn't think it's a good idea
to go after Chem Co.

                    TOM
Why not?

WALLACE

Because it is a David and Goliath story that
is unlikely to end well - despite biblical
precedent.

DALE

On the other hand, if you're innocent -

TOM

Of course I'm innocent, that's what I've
been trying to tell you. The whole thing
is a hoax, a con, there was no bomb.

WALLACE

You say. They say -

TOM

Look, they were storing volatile materials
together, petro-chemicals, nitrates, sodium
cyanide, storing them in a random fashion
instead of separately as they were supposed
to do. And all to save a buck on warehouse
storage space. So I filed a safety report.

WALLACE

Yes we -

TOM

After they ignored the third complaint, I
went over their heads and wrote to the
VIP's at HQ Houston. No one wanted to
know. I was downgraded and fired. Then
when the whole thing blew -

DALE

Tom -

TOM

Now we have five dead, including two fire-
fighters and a dozen injured. Not to mention
the release of toxins that poisoned the air and
water supply. They're looking at a pay out
in the billions, a pay out that could bankrupt
them - they'll have lawsuits coming out of
their ears -

DALE

Tom -

TOM

So they went looking for a fall guy. Someone
to pin it on, save their bacon. Ease the pain.

WALLACE
Chem Co. is not going to go bankrupt. It is a
multi-national company. It employs tens of
thousands worldwide. It is an enormous
source of revenue for the State and Federal
budgets as well as foreign governments. It
is too big to fail.

TOM
Tell me something I don't already know.

DALE
The professor is just suggesting -

WALLACE
I'm suggesting we stay away from a long,
drawn out battle with a giant multi-national
company if we can. I'm suggesting we sue
for a new trial on the basis of -

TOM
Yes, I got that.

WALLACE
The evidence against you -

TOM
Tell me about it.

WALLACE
- is compelling.

TOM
Ridiculous!

WALLACE
Even so -

TOM
Do you really think I would make this up?
I'm not that smart.

DALE
He's got a point.

        (Wallace and Dale stare at him
        as if he's deluded.)

TOM
Look, I don't blame you for being skeptical.
Believe me. I'm just as bewildered as you
are. The photos, the security footage...

TOM (cont'd)
the salacious junk on my computer - the
whole thing is amazing to me. It's like
I walked into the Fun House, you know,
with those weird mirrors and you look
completely distorted, unrecognizable...
Dale, you know me.

DALE
I thought I did.

TOM
Do you really believe that I fit this profile?
That I could do these things?

DALE
It doesn't matter. I'm only one vote and
my vote doesn't count.

TOM
It counts with me.

WALLACE
Mr. Yeager, you are not on trial here.

DALE
We're only trying to help.

WALLACE
i can see that you feel aggrieved by what
may very well be an unjust attack on your
character. But you'll get no satisfaction
by hammering away at it. In fact, it will
only drag you into a murky arena of
charge and counter charge. My advice is
to drop it - completely. It's a miasma
which will only cloud the air and make a
new trial or a mistrial legally impossible.

TOM
You don't believe me.

WALLACE
What we believe or don't believe is irrelevant.

TOM
Not to me.

WALLACE
If you are looking for some kind of personal
exoneration -

TOM

You bet I am. Why not?

WALLACE

It's a dead end. A wrong turn. Not only will
you get no satisfaction, but you will be
discrediting, perhaps unfairly, a lot of
upright, do right, individuals who -

TOM

I can't help that -

WALLACE

But you can help yourself - by not going
there. It's dark, it's messy, it's a swamp of
half truths, layer upon layer of intrigue, mis-
representation, and confusion that a lot of
people here invested in personally.

DALE

I know you, Tom. I know you wouldn't
want to falsely accuse anyone, as I'm sure
you have been accused. Good people,
perhaps, who have been misled. Innocent
people, like you. Do you really want to go
that route?

.   (Tom doesn't answer.)

DALE

Drop it. It's your only way out. You're only
exit.

(Tom looks to Wallace.)

TOM

You think there's a chance?

WALLACE

If we keep the argument simple, then yes.
You have a right to a fair trial. That's the
law. You didn't have one. There are grounds
for a new trial, the adverse publicity, the
denial of -

TOM

What about Chem Co? They'll raise hell?

WALLACE

Maybe not. Chem Co. wants this thing to
go away too. They don't want to be on
cable news for the next couple of years.

WALLACE (cont'd)

They don't want their dirty linen chewed
over on the front pages of the Wall Street
Journal.

TOM

No, they'll fight it. Down to the wire. There is
too much at stake. Not just the money. Their
reputation. They'll string it out. If they back off,
it will only be because it's in their interests to
back off. We'd have to give them a reason to
cash in their chips.

(The sound of a car pulling up
is heard.

Tom goes to the window and
looks out.)

DALE

What is it?

TOM

Can't see.

(KNOCK is heard. Dale starts
for the door.)

TOM

I'll go.

DALE

No, let me.

(She goes.)

WALLACE

Police?

TOM

I don't think so.

DALE (OFFSTAGE)

Yes?

MARCY'S VOICE

Hi. I'm Marcy Grier.

WALLACE
(to himself)

Oh no. Oh no, oh no.

                    TOM
What?

                MARCY'S VOICE
I'm looking for Preston Wallace.

                    TOM
What is it?

                  WALLACE
It's the end of the line.

                MARCY'S VOICE
Is he here?

                  WALLACE
          (calling)
It's alright, Dale!

          (Tom exits as the door slams
          and Dale and Marcy enter.)

                   MARCY
Professor! Thank God.

                  WALLACE
Ms Grier! What a - surprise.

                   MARCY
I've been trying to reach you. I thought
something might have happened to you.

                  WALLACE
No, just a phone problem. What is it?

                   MARCY
Obviously you haven't heard.

                  WALLACE
Heard what?

                   MARCY
Someone leaked Bolton's resignation to
the Press. The president wants to move
forward ASAP to avoid unnecessary
speculation.

                  WALLACE
Ms Grier, this is Dale Hardy.

                    DALE
Hello.

                    MARCY
Hi.

                    WALLACE
She's assisting me with - some legal work.

                    DALE
Would you like a drink?

                    MARCY
A juice would be great.

                    WALLACE
Scotch for me - if that's alright.

            (Dale exits.)

                    MARCY
We haven't much time. The president will make
the announcement from the Oval Office the
day after tomorrow.

            (Wallace stares.)

                    MARCY
Oh, I'm sorry. The - uh - nomination is yours -
if you still want it.

            (Pause. He hiccups.)

                    WALLACE
I'd be -

                    MARCY
Good. Congratulations.

                    WALLACE
I feel -

                    MARCY
Overwhelmed. Obviously.

                    WALLACE
That too.

                    MARCY
I brought along a couple of briefing books
so we can make a start.

                    WALLACE
A start?

MARCY

Prep for the committee.

WALLACE

Oh, yes.

(Marcy pulls two large three
ring binders from her shoulder
bag.)

WALLACE

It's all so sudden -

MARCY

Tell me about it. When I couldn't reach
you, I panicked.

WALLACE

Apologies again. It's been a bit chaotic
here as well.

MARCY

Really?

WALLACE

Yes. Been a bit - tied up, so to speak.

MARCY

Research?

WALLACE

Yes, as a matter of fact. Had my hands full.

MARCY

Well, never mind. I found you.

WALLACE

You did.

MARCY

To tell you the truth I was glad to get out of
Washington. SInce the leak, my phone
hasn't stopped ringing.

WALLACE

I bet.

(Dale enters with drinks.)

DALE

Here we are.

MARCY
(taking a drink)
Oh, thanks.
(toasting Wallace)
To you, professor!

DALE
Are we celebrating?

WALLACE
In a way.

DALE
Hang on. I'll get my drink.

(Dale exits.)

MARCY
Probably best to keep this between us
until - it's official.

WALLACE
Right. As a matter of fact it may be best to
hold off altogether.

MARCY
(bewildered)
Why?

WALLACE
There's been a - hiccup...a wrinkle.

MARCY
Nothing serious, I hope.

WALLACE
Could be.

MARCY
Scandalous?

WALLACE
No. At least - not yet.

MARCY
Why didn't you tell me?

WALLACE
I couldn't. I didn't know.

MARCY
Didn't know what?

                    WALLACE
I never dreamed -

                    MARCY
What? what is it?

                    WALLACE
It all just - happened.

                    MARCY
What happened for goodness sake?

        (Tom enters with a hammer.)

                    WALLACE
It's...
              (noticing Tom)
Tom

                    TOM
Hi.

                    WALLACE
Tom, this is Ms Grier from the - Justice
Department.

                    MARCY
Hi.

                    TOM
Hey.

                    WALLACE
Tom's been fixing the water pump on
my Cherokee...

        (Wallace looks to Dale who
        has entered with her drink.)

                    WALLACE
Dale. perhaps you could update Ms
Grier on the - situation?

            (Blackout.)

A MORE PERFECT UNION

ACT 2

Scene 2

A day later.

DALE and TOM and MARCY hold briefing
binders as they question WALLACE.

MARCY
Are you a strict constructionist? A judicial activist?
Originalist?

WALLACE
Well, I think if Chief Justice Marshall had been
asked his judicial philosophy, he would have been
hard pressed to sandwich himself into an answer
that would satisfy this committee.

MARCY
Are you stone walling or comparing yourself
to the Chief Justice.

WALLACE
Neither. Although -

MARCY
I like the reference to Marshall, but just make
sure you don't sound evasive. They hate that.

WALLACE
No, I -

MARCY
Can you expand? Help us out here.

WALLACE
Well, as you know, Justice Marshall in Marbury
vs. Madison, established the power of the
Supreme Court to say not only what the law
is, but also to strike down any law passed by
Congress that is repugnant to the Constitution.

MARCY
...the right of the Court to judicial review.

WALLACE
Yes. And that opinion has proven to be as
solid as the Constitution itself.

MARCY

But on what basis, in your view, does the
Court determine what might be repugnant
to the Constitution?

WALLACE

I would look to the text. Determine the
Framer's intent. How the law was understood
when it was ratified.

MARCY

So you are an Originalist?

WALLACE

No, no, I believe -

MARCY

It sounds like it to me.

WALLACE

No, Originalism, to my mind, holds that law
should be interpreted on the reading of the
text alone - that which is actually written down.

MARCY

Yes?

WALLACE

But that is not my view.

MARCY

You're heading into murky waters here,
professor. Can you clarify?

WALLACE

Well... the right of an unelected Court to
use unwritten law as a basis to strike down
properly enacted measures is open to
vigorous debate. The danger is that a judge
could gravitate toward a version of history
that suits their own beliefs about good vs
bad policy.

MARCY

For example?

WALLACE

Well, something like the law restricting
secession from the Union. It is not written
down, but implied. We fought a civil war
over that one. Or money is speech,
corporations are people.

(Marcy's phone hums. She checks
the caller ID and takes the call.)

WALLACE

Again, not written down but implied - both
now settled law, protected under the 1st
and 4th amendments.

MARCY (ON PHONE)

Yes.
      (to Wallace)
Sorry - go ahead.

WALLACE

So there is this pull within the Court to
determine what exactly the text of the
Constitution implies - relevant to a particular
case.

DALE

Determined how?

WALLACE

That is the debate. To my mind the intent of
the Framer's was to create a more perfect
Union. Does a law advance or weaken that
objective. That is the ultimate criteria. What
principle laid down in the Constitution are we
defending?

TOM

All men are created equal.

DALE

We the people.

WALLACE

Precisely. The underlying basis for all law
must be supported by a principle or it is not
law, and eventually, over time, will hopefully
be overturned.

MARCY (ON PHONE)

Okay. Let me know.

DALE

Still one man's principle is another man's
poison.

WALLACE

Yes, I think it was Justice Frankfurter who
said, "the Supreme Court was like nine
scorpions in a bottle..."

MARCY
(hanging up phone)
Could be right. When Justice Vinson died,
Frankfurter said that it was the first indica-
tion he ever had that there was a god.

(Wallace chuckles.)

MARCY
Still want the job, professor?

WALLACE
I take the 5th.
(referring to call)
What was that?

MARCY
They're looking into it...

(All eyes on Marcy.)

MARCY
It's evolving.

DALE
Oh - like women's rights.

MARCY
Let's hope.

DALE
We have the vote. We can own property.

MARCY
Only took a hundred years.
(to Wallace)
Is your daughter flying in for the hearings?

WALLACE
Depends.

MARCY
It would be helpful to have her there.

WALLACE
I'd like to see how things play out before I -

MARCY
Let's keep our focus then.

(Marcy's phone hums. She checks
the ID.)

MARCY (ON PHONE)
Hang on.
                    (rising)
I'll take this to the porch.
                    (to Dale and Tom)
Put him through his paces. No let up.
Campaign finance, gun control, privacy rights,
they'll be sure to raise these issues...
                    (exiting)
Back in a jiff.

          (Marcy exits.)

TOM
That's a hell of a phone she's got there.

DALE
What are your views on precedents?

WALLACE
How about a break?

DALE
No, this is important.

TOM
Tough as nails.

WALLACE
Is that true.

DALE
I'm a sweetheart.

WALLACE
I could use you in Washington.

TOM
She's getting job offers and I'm looking at
life - if I'm lucky.

DALE
Precedents.

WALLACE
Well, generally speaking, I think precedents
should be respected.

DALE
Oh, yes?

          (She waits.

WALLACE

...on the other hand if a precedent is blatantly
wrong and the opportunity arises, a precedent
can and should be overturned.

(Slight pause.)

DALE

For example?

WALLACE

Dred Scott. Also Lochner vs. New York, 1906,
Plessy vs. Ferguson, 1896 and so on.

TOM

Dred Scott?

WALLACE

The Taney Court ruled that slaves had no rights
and could never be citizens. It was struck down
after the civil war when Congress passed the
13th, 14th and 15th amendments.

TOM

So, in that case, it was Congress that
nullified the Court's ruling, not the Court
itself.

WALLACE

That's right.

TOM

What about Lochner?

WALLACE

Lochner was a worker's rights case, breath-
taking in its implications.

DALE

In what way?

WALLACE

The Court basically decided that all efforts to
protect workers or regulate the private market
were unconstitutional.

TOM

Struck sown?

WALLACE

Yes, by Congress - 30 years later.

DALE
Would you say that the opinion in Lochner
was a case of judicial activism?

WALLACE
I don't know if I would use that term in the
way it is understood today. Lochner was by
no means the only workers rights case to be
struck down. There was a raft of them.

TOM
Bummer.

WALLACE
Yes, it was pretty brutal.

(Tom hovers near the French
doors, trying to over hear Marcy.)

DALE
Brown vs. Board of Education, Topeka,
Kansas.

WALLACE
Brown overthrew the 'separate but equal'
clause established in Plessy.

DALE
On what grounds?

WALLACE
On the grounds that Plessy violated the
'equal' protection clause in the 14th
amendment.

TOM
And was repugnant to the Constitution.

WALLACE
Right.

DALE
Some have argued that Plessy was established
precedent and should have been left alone.

WALLACE
Well -

DALE
That it is not the obligation or the right of the
judicial branch to be making laws.

WALLACE
As I said, the Court does have the power
to strike down any law -

TOM
Marbury vs. Madison.

WALLACE
You were paying attention.

DALE
Yes, but some would say, and have said,
that Brown was judicial activism run riot.

WALLACE
It was a unanimous decision. Nine zip.

DALE
Still -

WALLACE
Some could also say, if it comes to it, that
both Plessy and Lochner were judicial
activism in reverse.

DALE
So now you're saying Lochner was judicial
activism?

WALLACE
Look, we're getting side tracked. Brown is
a landmark case, beyond precedent, almost
as solid as the Constitution itself. I don't think
it will come up before the committee.

DALE
What about Shelby vs Holder?

WALLACE
The Court invalidated the pre-clearance clause
in the 1965 Voting Rights Act.

DALE
Even though Congress reviewed the law on
several occasions and affirmed its validity.

WALLACE
What's your point?

DALE
Would you say that this was a case of judicial
activism?

WALLACE
Not if I hope to be confirmed.

TOM
Keeping above the fray, professor!

WALLACE
Trying.

TOM
You're a shoo in.

> (Marcy returns with phone in
> one hand, a small notebook in
> the other.)

MARCY
How's it going?

WALLACE
I'm being brow beaten.

TOM
What's up?

MARCY
Your case is becoming more complicated
by the minute. Not only is there a problem
of a big pay out by Chem Co. if there is a
retrial, but there is also an emerging national
security factor in the mix...

TOM
You're kidding me?

MARCY
No.

TOM
What kind of factor?

MARCY
Not exactly sure. Waiting to hear back from
Homeland Security and the 5th Circuit Court.

TOM
Homeland Security? Really?

MARCY
Yes.

                    TOM
Why? What for?

                    MARCY
I don't know. I thought you might.

                    TOM
No, no idea. I'm in the dark.

                    MARCY
They're looking at your service record.
Your 201 file.

                    TOM
I'm still shooting blanks.

                    MARCY
Is there anything in that file I should
know about?

                    TOM
No, no idea. I've never seen the file.

                    MARCY
You were honorably discharged?

                    TOM
You bet. With all the fruit salad.

                    MARCY
Nothing came up in the trial?

                    TOM
No, just the PTSD angle - trying to
label me as a crazy vet.

                    MARCY
Is there anything to drink? I'd love a drink.

                    DALE
I'll have a look.

          (Dale exits.)

                    MARCY
So there's no reason someone would want
to do a demolition job on you?

                    TOM
No way. No chance.

MARCY
What about the Norris Court Martial?

(Pause.)
TOM
What about it?

MARCY
You testified against Corporal Norris.

TOM
I had nothing to do with that. That whole
thing came down from Command.

MARCY
I'm just asking.

TOM
You think - ?

MARCY
I don't know what to think. What happened?

TOM
There was a patrol. One of the tracks hit an
IED. Took some casualties. A lot of fire
and smoke. Confusion. Then Norris saw
some dudes running away and opened up -
thinking, you know, they were - responsible
for the IED...I told the Court what I saw. That
was it.

MARCY
Norris was convicted?

TOM
Yeah

(Dale returns with a juice.)

MARCY
Thanks.

TOM
...but he got off with time served. Took
a "General Discharge".

MARCY
You know what he's doing now?

TOM
No idea.

MARCY

He's got his own Hedge Fund...on his way
to being a billionaire - like his grandfather.

TOM

Norris?

MARCY

Ever heard of the Norris Foundation?

TOM

Sure.

MARCY

His grandfather started it. A real family
man. Tribal. Take no prisoners type. The
type who can make a "General Discharge"
go away.

(Slight pause as they absorb it.)

TOM

Look, I wasn't the only witness. There
were others.

MARCY

Yes, I'm aware of that.

TOM

What?

MARCY

One was run over by a truck. The other
emigrated to Australia.

TOM

What are you saying?

MARCY

I'm saying it may have been pay back for
blowing the whistle on Norris.

TOM

I didn't. They came to me... What was I
supposed to do? Lie?

MARCY

Then filing a negative safety report on
Chem Co... well you can see where I'm going.

TOM

You think this Chem Co. thing was a set up?

MARCY

I don't have to tell you that there is a mind
set out there that might see your testimony
against Norris as treasonous.

TOM

Is this a joke? You know after 9/11, nobody
had to find me.

MARCY

I'm just saying -

TOM

I enlisted.

MARCY

Yes, I know.

TOM

Who are these people?
(anguished)
Who are these people?

MARCY

I'm just speculating here. I'm sure it's -

TOM

Then why is it being suggested that the
trial is a national security matter?

MARCY

Chem Co. is a subsidiary of Zenith. Zenith
makes billions from military contracts,
weapons research, you name it.

TOM

Are you saying the military green lighted
this whole thing?

MARCY

I'm saying nothing. Chem Co. may have
actually believed you planted the bomb.

TOM

There was no bomb...

MARCY

Even so - the evidence -

TOM

Manufactured! And an outfit like Zenith would
have the money and resources to do it.

                    MARCY
Without leaving a paper trail?

                    TOM
They could have farmed it out. Gone overseas.
It's a multi-national. No way to trace it back to
Chem Co. or Zenith.

                    MARCY
It's a stretch.

                    TOM
Not if Chem Co's legal team was in the dark.
They think they've got their man. They think
they're the good guys. And all the time they're
being conned.

          (Pause.)

                    WALLACE
Is the president aware of this new - wrinkle?

                    MARCY
Oh, yes.

                    WALLACE
And he still wants to - ?

                    MARCY
He needs someone who can be confirmed.
He thinks, and I think, he can muster the
votes to - push you over the top...that is if
you walk a judicially neutral line in the
hearings. Besides that - and you never heard
it from me, he feels that no one should have
a monopoly on military contracts, that it's a
threat to the Republic, and it wouldn't hurt to
remind Zenith that they are being watched.

                    WALLACE
So he's hoping to use Tom's situation to
cut Zenith down to size?

                    MARCY
And to shine a light on any black ops under-
taken, past or present. It's a risk. But the
president wants to play it out - for awhile.

                    DALE
How long?

MARCY

The Court is divided. The professor, if confirmed, would be the swing vote and frankly
there's no one in the wings. Our other possibilities
could be contentious. We could lose in committee.
Look at what happened to Bork. Kennedy's been
a good Justice, but far from Reagan's first choice.
If Bork had been confirmed he would have altered
the direction of the Court.

WALLACE

Well, as far as that goes, I offer no guarantees.

MARCY

No one's asking that.

WALLACE

Alright then.

MARCY

On the other hand he doesn't want to be over-
heard saying years later, as Eisenhower said
about Earl Warren, that "it was the biggest
damn fool thing he ever did."

(Her phone hums.)

MARCY

Be right back.

(Marcy exits. Pause.)

TOM
(rising restlessly)
Now what?

(Dale looks anxiously at him then
reverts to her briefing book.)

DALE
(from book)
Do you believe that corporations are people?

(Wallace groans.)

WALLACE

Please. No more.

DALE
Could you expand? Or is that a yes?

                    TOM
                (to himself)
This Norris thing -

                    WALLACE
What was the question?

                    DALE
Corporations.

                    TOM
There was pressure sure, but nobody said -

                    DALE
Do you believe they are people? And as
such have rights under the equal protection
clause of the 14th amendment?

                    WALLACE
That's two questions.

                    DALE
Take your pick.

                    TOM
One minute I'm being offered the moon to
re-enlist... the next -

                    WALLACE
Santa Clara County vs Southern Pacific.

                    TOM
...it's take a hike.

                    DALE
A tax case.

                    WALLACE
Right.

                    WALLACE
The County taxed the fences running
along the tracks. The Court deemed the tax
unconstitutional.

                    TOM
Looks like someone wanted to cut me loose.

                    DALE
Unconstitutional on what grounds?

WALLACE
The Equal Protection Clause.

TOM
And they've been on my case ever since.

DALE
So corporations became people?

WALLACE
Not in the Court's written opinion.

DALE
But implied?

WALLACE
In a head note. But over the years - it has been
accepted as precedent.

DALE
So corporations evolved into people? Kind
of like Darwin.

WALLACE
More or less.

DALE
And money became speech, protected under
1st amendment - which led to unlimited
corporate money being used in campaign
financing.

TOM
Hell, I didn't even know this guy, Norris.

DALE
(to Tom)
Will you stop mumbling.

TOM
Who?

DALE
You. Who else?

TOM
I'm -

DALE
Going to grab a briefing book and give
me a hand.

WALLACE
Maybe we should take a break.

DALE
No!

WALLACE
Tom's - distracted. I'm exhausted -

DALE
We can do his life later. RIght now we are
drilling you on precedents so you can maybe
become a Supreme and save his bacon.

WALLACE
Even if I make the Court, it takes a con-
sensus to get a case reviewed -

TOM
What about the Appeal? The 5th Circuit?
Are we assuming that isn't going to happen?

WALLACE
No one's assuming anything.

TOM
Right.

(Wallace shrugs. Pause.)

DALE
They came to the house.

TOM
Who?

DALE
Two men.

TOM
When?

DALE
Years ago. They'd been reading our letters.

TOM
Why?

DALE
I don't know. They talked to dad. After - dad
told me to stop writing to you...said the war
had changed you...not the same.

                    TOM
And you believed it?

                    DALE
They had pictures.

                    TOM
What kind of pictures?

                    DALE
Probably the same kind they showed
at your trial.

                    TOM
You mean phony ones.

          (Dale nods.)

                    DALE
I think it broke dad's heart...excuse me.

          (Dale exits. After a moment Tom,
          in shock, sits and picks up the
          briefing book.)

                    TOM
In the gun case, D.C. vs. Heller, the
Courtr ruled for Heller.

                    WALLACE
I really think -

                    TOM
No, I want to do this.

                    WALLACE
                 (tentatively)
...Heller essentially reinterpreted the
2nd amendment right to bear arms to
include the right to own a handgun.

                    TOM
Reinterpreted how?

                    WALLACE
Well, its original intent was to protect the
country from a potential tyrannical government by allowing states to maintain militias.

          (Dale appears unseen, dabbing
          her eyes with a tissue.)

WALLACE

Prior to Heller the 'right to bear arms' was not considered a universal right. Heller overturned years of precedents.

DALE

Correctly?

(Tom looks up.)

TOM

Careful now, professor. Don't let her corner you.

WALLACE

I would say -

TOM

Nothing. Be smart. Walk the line.

WALLACE

Which is - ?

TOM

Heller is a landmark case. Established law. Leave it alone.

DALE
(sitting)
Was Heller judicial activism?

WALLACE

That's a judgment I'm not prepared to make.

TOM

Thank you.

DALE

But it's an issue that needs -

TOM

What about privacy rights? The clock is ticking and the professor has a plane to catch. - maybe.

DALE
(picking up briefing book)
Okay.

WALLACE

Privacy rights.

DALE

The thing that is tearing the country apart,
the thing that is an anathema to some, and
a sacred cow to others is the expansion of
privacy rights under the 4th amendment..

TOM

Miscegenation, same sex marriage,
contraception, abortion -

DALE

Search and seizure, surveillance, GPS
tracking, DNA collection...All cases that
have come before the Court.

TOM

Marcy thinks it's an area that might trip you
up on your way to being a Supreme.

WALLACE

And how do you suggest I avoid being -

DALE

Be alert.

TOM

Expect the worst. Someone is going to
throw you a curve, a slider, or even a bean ball.

DALE

No baseball references, please.
              (to Wallace)
Tom was a catcher in high school.

WALLACE

Ah.

TOM

All I'm saying is that this isn't going to be
a walk in the park. It's a blood sport.

WALLACE

You think privacy rights -

TOM

Trip wires - all.

WALLACE
              (with faint smile)
So how do I, in your opinion, handle these -
trip wires?

DALE

Stick to the Constitution.

TOM

Established law.

DALE

Precedents.

TOM

Framer's intent.

DALE

For example, Justice Brandeis said that
privacy rights are -
(reading)
"the most comprehensive right and the
most valued by civilized man..."

(Slight pause.)

TOM

"To protect that right - "

DALE

Excuse me.

TOM

Sorry I thought -

DALE

"To protect that right every unjustifiable
intrusion by the government upon the
privacy of an individual - must be deemed
a violation of the 4th amendment."

TOM

Done?

DALE

Done.

TOM

Anyway, you get the drift.

WALLACE

I do. Thank you.

TOM

We just don't want to see you crash and
burn up there.

(Marcy enters.)

                    MARCY
Okay, here's the deal. A counsel from Justice
clerked for one of the Supremes on the 5th
Circuit Court. Counsel asked for a cursory review.
The Justice had a quick look at your Appeal and
does think there are grounds for a retrial based
on pre-trial prejudice...If that vote holds, all you'll
need is one more.

                    DALE
Only one?

                    MARCY
It's a three judge panel.

                    WALLACE
Even if all three agree, Chem Co's legal
team could ask for a full nine judge review.

                    MARCY
They could, yes.

                    TOM
Seems thin.

                    MARCY
There's no guarantee. I don't want to sugar coat it...
But we're betting they won't. The genie is out of the
bottle. Chem Co. knows that Justice is looking into
their operation and that things could go south for
them. We think their parent company, Zenith, will
pass on a full review and risk a retrial. No blame, no
shame. Everyone goes back to the drawing board.
Tom gets a good defense lawyer. Justice might help
with that.. I know it's a gamble, but it's all we can do.

                    TOM
What if I lose?

                    MARCY
You can always petition the Supreme Court.
If the professor is confirmed, you'll have
at least one vote.

                    DALE
Let's hope it doesn't come to that.

                    WALLACE
Let's hope.

MARCY

You'd have to give yourself up, of course. But
not here, not in this State. There can be no
connection to the professor.

WALLACE

It's too big a risk. I'd rather withdraw now than
take a chance on Tom's spending years in jail.

TOM

What's the matter, professor? Don't you trust
our legal system? We the people...all men
are created equal.

WALLACE

Of course.

TOM

Then there's no choice.

(All eyes on Tom.)

TOM

If you make the Court, you might have a
chance to perfect the Union, to do something most of us can only dream of doing,
effect the lives of millions. I can't stand in the
way even if your chances are slim to none. If
i go down, I'm not going to drag you with me...
So go. Go back to Washington. Study up with
the pros and be a Supreme. I'll live with the
Appeal.

(Pause.)

DALE

You sure?

(Tom nods.)

MARCY

That's it then.

(Blackout.)

C SPAN COMMENTATOR (V.O.)

"...just waiting for the hearings to begin. The
nominee, Judge Preston Wallace, has taken
his seat, now nodding to his daughter, who
has apparently flown in from Vienna where
she is an exchange student, to offer her support."

A MORE PERFECT UNION

ACT 3

Scene 3

MOTEL ROOM

> Lights up on Tom and Dale watching an
> unseen TV screen. He mutes the sound.

                    TOM
          (after a moment)
How about I change my mind? Do a runner?

                    DALE
          (incredulous)
You're not really thinking of...

          (He doesn't respond.)

                    DALE
Tom?

                    TOM
No. Just nervous.

                    DALE
Then don't torture me.

          (She punches him.)

                    TOM
What time is it?

          (Dale checks her watch.)

                    DALE
Almost time...

                    TOM
They'll be here any minute.

                    DALE
There should be time to catch his opening
statement.

                    TOM
What if the Feds get lost? Don't show?
          (off her look)
I didn't mean to torture you. I was just -

                    DALE

Well, stop it...you've always tortured me.

                    TOM

You say.

                    DALE

Always.

                    TOM

With a little help from my friends.

                    DALE

Oh yes...that.

                    TOM

Pretty disappointing, I bet.

                    DALE

Yes...it was.

                    TOM

Never mind. All phony baloney.

          (Dale nods, unable to speak.)

                    TOM

I should sue for alienation of your
affections.

          (She smiles through her tears.)

                    DALE

You'd lose.

          (Pause. He takes her hand.)

                    TOM

I've always been your biggest fan.

                    DALE

Hah!

          (She pulls her hand away.)

                    TOM

Since you were ten.

                    DALE

That's a laugh.

                    TOM
You could run faster than me. You could
pass and catch. You played tackle, not
touch football.

                    DALE
That was my big attraction?

                    TOM
At ten, yes...later...

                    DALE
Don't bring up later. It's not politic.

                    TOM
Later there was holding hands in the
picture show.

                    DALE
My first mistake.

                    TOM
You've always been different - unique.

                    DALE
You say.

                    TOM
Who else plays tackle football at ten. No
one does that.

                    DALE
You said that already. I'm waiting for you
to move on to other - assets.

                    TOM
You were very good with the professor.
Really put him through his paces.

                    DALE
Well, I was a paralegal -

                    TOM
I think he was really impressed the way you
handled the briefing. If he gets confirmed,
he'll have you to thank.

                    DALE
You think?

                    TOM
Absolutely. You put him on the spot. Pinned
him down.

                    DALE
I think he was getting annoyed with me.
Quoting Brandeis...

                    TOM
Not a chance.

                    DALE
I don't know.

                    TOM
He practically offered you a job... and that's
just for starters.

                    DALE
You say.

                    TOM
I do say...you should think about it.

                    DALE
What? D.C.?

                    TOM
Hmm... you might meet the president.

                    DALE
You think?

                    TOM
You'd have a shot. Those Supremes do
the party circuit. He'd need someone on
his arm - someone to keep the conversation
going. You're good at that.

                    DALE
Am I?

                    TOM
You've always had the gift of the gab.

                    DALE
This is my strong suit?

          (Pause.)

                    DALE
Anyway, I couldn't take Danny out of school.

TOM

It'd be an education. He could see all the
monuments...Mount Vernon, the Lincoln
Memorial...

DALE

He has all his friends here.

TOM

He'd make new friends.

DALE

If I left, you wouldn't know where to find
me...

(They look at each other...then
a long desperate embrace.)

DALE

I think they're starting.

TOM
(holding her)
Wait. I want to - to thank you.

DALE

Is that what this is?

TOM

No, listen...I want to say this now -

DALE

Tom -

TOM

I don't know how this will play out...
but...whatever happens - just wanted you
to know how grateful I am for putting me
up - and all the rest - the risk...I -

DALE

Oh, well -

TOM

It was above and beyond -

DALE

Well -

TOM

Really.

DALE

I'm glad, in a way, that you came - to me.
That you thought...

TOM

I thought of no one else. Funny, isn't it.
Out of the blue. On the run. And it came
to me -

DALE

Yes, it is funny.

(Slight pause.)

DALE

If the Appeal goes through - you might make
bail.

TOM

You think?

DALE

Marcy's lining up a lawyer on the off chance -
you know - that you get a new trial.

TOM

It's Chem Co. that should be on trial.

DALE

They will be...Zenith too.

TOM

Who knows? Maybe there won't even
be a trial.

DALE

You serious?

TOM

Trial deferred. "Chem Co, too big to fail,
has reluctantly dropped its case against
alleged bomber, Tom Yeager, at the request
of Homeland Security."

DALE

You're fantasizing.

TOM

Anything is possible. I mean if this whole
thing hadn't happened, I wouldn't be here.
Wouldn't have seen you again.

                              DALE
There you go - perhaps not equal compen-
sation, but -

                              TOM
You say...I say you're the one.

                              DALE
I always thought so...

                              TOM
We're like the Constitution.

                              DALE
How's that?

                              TOM
Moving toward a more perfect Union.

                              DALE
You mean - striking down bad precedents.

                              TOM
And insuring domestic tranquility.

                              DALE
Establishing justice.

                              TOM
Promoting the general welfare.

                              DALE
Securing the blessings of liberty.

          (There is a KNOCK on the door.

                              TOM
                    (glancing at TV)
Hey, it's started.

          (He un-mutes the sound.)

                         WALLACE (V.O.)
It has been said we are a nation of laws,
not people.

          (A second KNOCK more insistent.)

                              TOM
Yeah! Coming!

          (Tom looks to Dale, then exits.)

WALLACE (V.O.)
Some have referred to the Constitution as a
civic religion.

(Dale watches the TV momentarily.)

WALLACE (V.O.)
We are Americans to the degree that we adhere
to these constitutional laws, laws that are based
on time honored principles.

DALE
Tom!...Tom?

(Dale exits quickly.)

Lights cross fade and come up on
Wallace in a spotlight.)

WALLACE
My hope, if I am confirmed by this committee
and the Senate, is to be, to the best of my ability,
an advocate for these principles, that they may
enlighten my decisions.

Solomon, in the Old Testament, prayed for
wisdom that he might judge so great a people. I
pray like- wise, for wisdom, that I might judge so
great a country. A country whose laws, written in
the aftermath of cannon and fire, created a
nation, as Lincoln said, "conceived in liberty and
dedicated to the proposition that all men are
created equal".

I feel that if we, the people, in this room and in this
country, adhere to that proposition, this nation
will not perish from the earth. And to that end, I,
for one, dedicate my heart and my life... I thank you
for your consideration and welcome your questions.

(Lights fade to black.)

THE END

Printed in Great Britain
by Amazon

17075002R00131